ISLAND WITHIN A CITY

ISLAND WITHIN A CITY

THOMAS McGOWEN

A History of the Norridge-Harwood Heights Area

EISENHOWER PUBLIC LIBRARY DISTRICT
Harwood Heights, Illinois

The Eisenhower Public Library District, Harwood Heights, IL

© 1989 by The Eisenhower Public Library District. All rights reserved.
Published 1989
Printed in the United States of America

DEDICATION

To past and present citizens of the area, who made this history that is our roots.

To future citizens of the area, who will read this history and come to better understand the roots of their community.

CONTENTS

Page

Chapter 1   INDIAN DAYS: 1776-1835   1

Chapter 2   THE FIRST SETTLERS: 1835-1860   17

Chapter 3   WAR, CATASTROPHE, AND LOCAL
POLITICS: 1861-1899   31

Chapter 4   FROM FARM COMMUNITY TO GROWING
SUBURB: 1900-1945   47

Chapter 5   THE BIRTH AND GROWTH OF THE TWO
VILLAGES: 1946-1959   69

Chapter 6   MOVING INTO MODERN TIMES: 1960-1980's   97

Bibliography   137

Index   139

FOREWORD

Ideas become realities through the efforts of people's special interest and dedication. Recording the history of the villages of Norridge and Harwood Heights had been in the minds and on the lips of local residents for many years. As the ranks of older citizens of the area began to dwindle, the urgency for both an oral and written local history increased.

About a decade ago, under the auspices of the Eisenhower Library, efforts commenced to translate the idea of a written local history into a reality. It was fitting that the impetus for a written history should come from the trustees of the library who served both Norridge and Harwood Heights.

Island Within A City is the culmination of a community idea. Author Thomas McGowen, himself a longtime resident of the community, presents in this volume a history of the two villages. McGowen's lively text traces events of early Indian days (1776-1835) to modern times (1980's). His narrative weaves into the fabric of regional and national history local events, people, and places.

The purpose of this volume is to provide a panoramic view of the past so that those who read *Island Within A City* will have a better understanding of the roots of our villages.

Persons whose interest extend beyond the scope of this book are invited to peruse the vertical files on local history preserved at the Eisenhower Library and to consult with the library staff for additional sources regarding the history of Norridge and Harwood Heights.

JOSEPH A. PATRICELLI, *President*
Eisenhower Public Library District
September, 1986

ACKNOWLEDGEMENTS

Present and former members of the Eisenhower Public Library District Board of Trustees: Ruth Igoe, Gary Ross, Natalie Rothbart, Dennis Enright, Catherine Kupczyk, Lucille Adamick, Irwin Rappaport, Joseph Patricelli and Martin Schneider, for their pursuit of local history; Don Johnson and Martin Schneider for collecting and compiling information contained in this book and in the library's local history files; Violet Rosier for typing and proofreading; Ron Stoch and Tom Heller for photography work; and the many people who live in Norridge, Harwood Heights and the surrounding areas, who have shared their photographs, memories and themselves, to make this book possible.

Special thanks to Norwood Park Township and the Villages of Norridge and Harwood Heights for their support of this local history project, especially their monetary contributions.

CHAPTER 1

INDIAN DAYS: 1776-1835

INDIAN DAYS: 1776-1835

AT THE TIME when the United States of America came into existence with the Declaration of Independence, the area that now includes the communities of Harwood Heights and Norridge was an open wilderness—a section of flat prairie dotted with marshy patches, out of which rose two low narrow hills, or ridges, with clusters of oak trees around them. In summer, this area was a sea of six-foot high yellow grass, interspersed with millions of pink, yellow, and blue flowers, through which grazing buffalo often plodded. In winter, it was generally an expanse of sparkling, pure white snow.

To the north, the prairie extended for a number of miles until it ran into deep forest. To the west, it extended for only a mile or so until it came to the river that French explorers had named the Aux Plaines, but which would become known as the Des Plaines. A shallow forest of hickories, cottonwoods, bur oaks, maples and elms spread out a ways from both its banks, but beyond it the prairie stretched on for countless miles into the heartland of the continent. To the east, the prairie continued for several miles and then bumped into another river; the clear little stream that was the north branch of the Chicago. It, too, had shallow woods running along both its banks, but beyond the woods on the east bank, instead of more prairie, lay wind-blown sand dunes that surrounded the great lake we now call Michigan. The stream flowed south several miles, joined with another stream—the Chicago's south branch—and together they sent a broad finger of water winding around a sandy hill to pour into the lake. A few miles to the south, a twelve-mile wide area of mucky, marshy swampland ran from the south branch of the Chicago westward to the Des Plaines.

In 1776 this entire region was the land of the native American people known to us as the Potawatomi Indians. They had several small villages in the area, and one lay beside the river that fed into the lake, and which they called *checagou;* meaning, apparently, something like "where the strong-

3

smelling onions grow," because of the numerous patches of smelly wild onions that thrived along the riverbanks. The lake they called *mishi-gonong*—"place of great water". They lived in dome-shaped huts formed of a number of slim, young, peeled tree trunks, stuck in the ground in a circle, bent over and tied together at the tops, and covered with sheets of tree bark.

With spears and arrows tipped with sharp points of chipped flintstone, Potawatomi men hunted deer, squirrels, raccoons and porcupines in the woods, and ducks, geese, and other waterfowl in the swampland—and it is a certainty that bands of Potawatomi hunters, on their way to try to kill one of the buffalo that drifted in vast herds back and forth across the prairie, often trod upon ground that is now criss-crossed by the streets of Norridge and Harwood Heights, and that their evening campfires often glowed in places where houses and apartment buildings now stand.

In the summertime, on little patches of ground beside their huts, Pota-watomi women grew little crops of corn, squash, beans, and tobacco, which the men smoked in pipes with ground-out stone bowls and carved wooden stems. The women also gathered wild rice from the rivers, and raspberries, blackberries, and other wild fruits in the woods. In the spring they tapped maple trees for maple syrup, which the Potawatomis used in much the same way as we use ketchup and mustard—as a condiment, to give flavor to many kinds of foods.

The Potawatomis of the region were well-off and peaceful. They were friendly toward the European explorers and trappers that came into the area from time to time beginning in the 1600's. In the 1770's, a dark-skinned

Example of what prairie land looked like in what was to become Norridge-Harwood Heights.

The bark-covered Algonquian summer house was a traditional type of dwelling used by the Potawatomis and other tribes in the Old Northwest.

Photo courtesy National Archives.

Spear fishing by torchlight was a fishing technique of the Potawatomi Indians and was probably often practiced on the Des Plaines River, in the Norridge-Harwood Heights area. *Photo courtesy Royal Ontario Museum.*

foreigner by the name of Jean Baptiste Point du Sable even came, with his family, and lived among them, building a log-cabin trading post near where the *checagou* flowed into the *mishigonong*. The Potawatomis traded him the furred skins of animals they hunted and trapped in return for muskets, ammunition, trinkets, and foodstuffs such as potatoes, salt, sugar, and whiskey. Du Sable gradually expanded his operation until, by the year 1800, it included a large, well-furnished house, stables, barns, and several other buildings. But for some reason, Du Sable then sold all this to another trader named Jean La Lime, and went elsewhere.

The Potawatomis accepted La Lime, and the few other traders that trickled into the area, as they had accepted Du Sable. But then, one day, a large group of pale-skinned men all dressed much alike, came into the area and began cutting down trees to build a fortress of logs not far from La Lime's place. It was the year 1803, the men were soldiers of the United States Army, and they were building what was to be Fort Dearborn, which marked a point on the new western boundary of the United States.

When the fort was finished, more soldiers, some with their families, came to occupy it. More traders and trappers arrived, among them a former Canadian by the name of John Kinzie, who bought the old Du Sable place from La Lime.

The Potawatomis were not particularly happy about this sudden large-scale invasion of paleskins, and as time went on, many of them became more and more hostile to the newcomers. This hostility was encouraged by British

Indian Burial Ground, by George Winter. The miniature grave house in Winter's painting was commonly used by the Potawatomis in their burials.

Photo courtesy Tippecanoe County Historical Society.

6

Chicago in 1779, showing the cabin of Jean Baptiste Point de Sable, the first permanent settler. Engraving by Raoul Varin, published by Ackermann and Sons, Paris, France, 1930. *Photo courtesy Chicago Historical Society.*

agents operating out of Canada, who hoped to block United States expansion into the area. They gave the Potawatomis muskets, ammunition, presents, and promises, and when it became obvious that the United States and Great Britain would soon be at war, they urged the Potawatomis to come in on their side—to attack the fort and drive the paleskinned Americans out of Potawatomi territory!

The war broke out in the summer of 1812. Almost at once, United States forces suffered bad defeats, losing forts on Mackinac Island and at what is now Detroit. In panic, the commander of United States forces in the west decided that Fort Dearborn couldn't be held against a British attack from Canada, and should be abandoned. He ordered the fort's commander, Captain Nathan Heald, to give away all the fort's trade goods to friendly Indians, to dump all the extra ammunition and the quantities of liquor into the river, and to take all the fort's soldiers and civilians back eastward to the nearest U.S. military installation, Fort Wayne (now the city of Fort Wayne, Indiana). An army officer who was a skilled frontiersman, Captain William Wells, was sent from Fort Wayne with thirty friendly Indians of the Miami tribe, to help with the evacuation of Fort Dearborn and the protection of its people.

Perhaps if Captain Heald had abandoned the fort at once, everything would have been all right. But he spent days talking things over with his officers, with Kinzie and some of the other traders, and with a number of Potawatomis who were friendly to the people of the United States. While

7

this was going on, word leaked out to the Potawatomis that the fort was to be abandoned, and the braves who wanted war were overjoyed. They had hesitated to attack the fort as their British friends had urged, but now their enemies were going to come right out among them. Bands of Potawatomis as well as warriors from more distant tribes, began to make their way to Fort Dearborn.

Kinzie and the other traders, most of the officers, and all of the friendly Potawatomis had urged Captain Heald not to leave the fort, but Heald finally decided that he had to obey his orders. He called a meeting of all the local Indian leaders and announced that the fort was being abandoned and all the soldiers and most of the traders were leaving. Some of the Potawatomi chiefs immediately insisted that their warriors would furnish an escort to help their white friends leave in peace and safety—words that must have brought sneers to the faces of Kinzie, Wells, and others who knew of the Potawatomis' true feelings of hatred for the paleskinned Americans.

On the 13th of August, Heald opened up the storehouse and gave away the government trade goods of blankets, cloth, paint, and other things to the groups of Indians that were now camped all around the fort. However, the air reeked with the tang of all the whiskey that the soldiers had poured into the river, and the Indians, who loved and craved this strong drink, were furious that it, too, hadn't been given to them.

A view of the original Fort Dearborn. Engraving. ©1897 by George M. Fergus.
Photo courtesy Chicago Historical Society.

On the morning of August 15, a typical simmering-hot Illinois summer day, the wooden gates of Fort Dearborn creaked open and a procession came winding out. Sixty some soldiers marched in ranks with a few officers on horseback alongside them; nine women and eighteen children rode in covered army supply wagons; and at the head of the column was Wells and his thirty Miamis, all on horseback. The procession turned south, moving among the sand dunes. A horde of Potawatomi braves, posing as an escort, began to move alongside it.

It is safe to say that most of the people from the fort were badly worried and some were probably terrified. Although they must have all been desperately hoping that the Potawatomis really *would* just act as an escort, most of them must have felt that they were surely going to die. Captain Wells, who had been brought up among the Miamis and followed many of their ways, had painted his face black, as the men of many Indian tribes did when they expected death or disaster.

The procession had gone no more than a mile and a half when the Potawatomi braves turned, and with a sudden shrill din of howling war whoops, attacked. The Miamis instantly rode off. The soldiers and some of the women fought, but they were, of course, badly outnumbered. In a matter of minutes, fifty-five men, two women, and twelve children were slaughtered. Five of the women, the rest of the children, and five men, were taken captive. The Potawatomis then burned the fort to the ground, after first thoroughly looting it. That night, they tortured the five captive American men to death.

Rebecca Wells Heald, the wife of Captain Nathan Heald, survived and was rescued by Alexander Robinson. No date, daguerreotype.
Photo courtesy Chicago Historical Society.

There are differing accounts of what happened during the massacre and in the days that followed, but according to one account that seems most accurate, Captain Heald and his wife, John Kinzie and his family, and a few of the others were saved by friendly Potawatomis who managed to get them away. The Healds and an army sergeant named Griffith were taken by canoe across the lake (to what is now the state of Michigan) to the home of an American fur trader named William Burnett. This, too, was Potawatomi country, but Burnett was able to stay safely among them because he was married to the daughter of a powerful Potawatomi chief. However, Burnett was fearful that the Healds and Griffith might be taken from him by some of the hostile Indians, so he and Heald hired a man to take the Healds and Griffith to a place where they would be completely safe.

The man they hired was a man who is now one of the foremost historical legends of the Norridge-Harwood Heights area. He was known to the Potawatomis as Che Che Pin Qua, a sort of nickname that meant "the squinter," or, "blinking eye".

Although he lived among the Potawatomis he was not a Potawatomi himself, being the son of an Ottawa mother and British father, but inasmuch as the Ottawa people were close allies of the Potawatomis, the Potawatomis accepted him as one of them. Che Che Pin Qua had visited the Fort Dearborn area several times and was well-known to John Kinzie and other traders

Alexander Robinson, or Che Che Pin Qua, in middle age, when he was living in what was to become the Norridge-Harwood Heights area.
Photo courtesy Chicago Historical Society.

there, who called him by the name his father apparently had given him, Alexander Robinson.

Robinson and two trustworthy Potawatomis took the Healds and Griffith by canoe up Lake Michigan to Mackinac Island, which lies far up near the tip of what is now Michigan state. It was a twenty-four day journey by canoe, and a dangerous one because of the strong winds that often suddenly spring up over the lake. The U.S. fort on the island had been captured by the British and was now manned by British soldiers, so the Healds and Griffith became prisoners of war, but they were well-treated and, at last, were completely safe.

When Robinson returned to his home, he found that a second group of Fort Dearborn refugees had been brought into the region; John Kinzie and his family and the wife of one of the Fort Dearborn officers. Robinson took these people into his home for several months until things had quieted down enough so that they were able to make their way up to Detroit, which was also in British hands.

The land around the burnt ruins of Fort Dearborn was now once again completely in Potawatomi hands; there were no U.S. citizens anywhere near

The old Kinzie house, the first house built in Chicago. The house was located near the southeast corner of Pine and Kinzie Streets. At left is Antoine Ouilmette's log house. Chromolithograph undated.

Photo courtesy Chicago Historical Society.

for many miles. In 1814, Alexander Robinson chose to bring his Potawatomi wife, known as Cynthia, and his children, across the lake and settled at what is now approximately the corner of Kinzie and Dearborn streets in Chicago. Together with a half-Potawatomi, half-French man named Antoine Ouilmette (after whom the city of Wilmette is named) he began to farm nearby, on fields that had been used by the soldiers of Fort Dearborn to grow wheat and vegetables.

The war between the United States and Great Britain officially came to an end in February of 1815, and the Potawatomis of the lands around Lake Michigan and the Chicago River quickly saw that the paleskins had not left for good after all. In the early summer of 1816 a company of U.S. soldiers came marching back to the site of Fort Dearborn, made camp, and began building a new fort. With soldiers to protect them, traders and others came trickling back into the area. John Kinzie and his family returned to their home, and Kinzie became trading agent for the new fort, which was also known as Fort Dearborn.

There was no more trouble from the Potawatomis. They could no longer count on any help from the British and it was obvious that they couldn't stand up against the United States on their own. They would have to make the best of things and learn to live with the paleskins, it seemed. However, the "paleskins" had other ideas.

In 1818, Illinois became the twenty-first state of the union. People continued to trickle into the area and settle in the little community around Fort

Engraving of Daniel Pope Cook (1795-1827) for whom Cook County is named.
Photo courtesy Chicago Historical Society.

Dearborn, which was now generally known by the name of "Chicago". Most of these people were easterners from New England states, some were immigrants from Europe, especially Germany. They had come to settle on new land here, on what was the nation's western frontier.

But there were already people on most of that land—the Potawatomis. Even before the war, U.S. government agents had been buying up land from groups of Illinois Indians, and this was now stepped up. Small groups of Potawatomis around the Chicago area were persuaded to give up parts of the land where they hunted, fished and trapped, in return for large amounts of trade goods such as clothing, tools, and food, and for the promise of yearly payments of money. These agreements between the Indians and the U.S. government were called treaties.

And so, the Chicago community was able to slowly grow. In 1831, Cook county was formed around it, named after Daniel Pope Cook, Illinois' second congressman. In 1833, Chicago, now with a population of 150 people, officially became a "village".

But the broad prairie region all around it, such as the place that would one day be Harwood Heights and Norridge, was still in the hands of Indians, and there were people in Chicago who couldn't wait to get out and settle on what looked to be good farmland. It was finally decided that one gigantic treaty should be worked out, that would once-and-for-all take over all the lands of the Potawatomi, Ottawa, and Chippewa people still in the area. The people of these tribes were called on to come to Chicago in the autumn of 1833 and sign the great treaty.

The Indians knew there was nothing they could do. They came by the thousands and camped on the prairielands, among the sand dunes, and at the edges of the woods, all around the little village. They came into Chicago, where the government representatives were waiting for them—along with whiskey peddlers, horse dealers, swindlers, and thieves, who saw the chance to make a fortune at such a huge gathering. The governor of Illinois, George B. Porter, was present, and made a speech in which he told the Indians that the "Great Father in Washington had heard that they wished to sell their lands." A Potawatomi chief called out that the Great Father in Washington must have met a bad bird that had told him a lie, for they didn't wish to sell what was left of their lands, they wished to keep them.

But the government agents argued, explained, wheedled, offered bribes, bought drinks of whiskey, and finally got their way. The final terms, which sounded reasonably good, were that the Indians would be given five million acres of land across the Mississippi River (in what is now Kansas and Oklahoma), the government would help them move to the new land, and would

13

make yearly payments of thousands of dollars for the building of new houses, schools, etc.

The Indians knew they really had no choice. They finally agreed.

A large number of them left the state right away. More went in 1834, and the last left in 1835. But several hundred of the last to go staged a kind of "goodbye dance" through the streets of Chicago before they went. Painted red and black, as if for war, they went whooping and howling and twisting and leaping through the town, making angry faces and threatening gestures at every paleskin they saw. Today, this would probably be called a protest demonstration. By nightfall it was over, and the village was quiet.

The Indian days of Illinois were ended, and the time of the settlers had come. The land that had belonged to the Chicago-area Potawatomis was now open and inviting. The section of prairie beyond the two ridges, where Norridge and Harwood Heights would someday exist, lay waiting for its new occupants.

The Farewell War Dance in 1835.

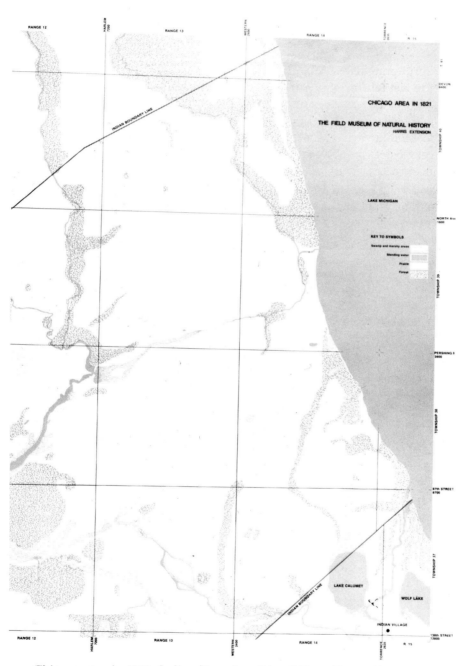

Chicago area in 1821. Indian Boundary Line follows Forest Preserve Drive at Harlem Avenue. *Photo courtesy Field Museum.*

CHAPTER 2

THE FIRST SETTLERS: 1835-1860

THE FIRST SETTLERS: 1835-1860

IN 1835 Chicago was only six miles square, with a population of 450 people, many of whom were apparently just waiting for the chance to move out onto the prairie. When the U.S. Government opened a land office on Lake Street near Clark and began offering properties that were now for sale throughout northern Illinois, the office was quickly swamped with buyers, a number of whom were interested in the Norridge-Harwood Heights area.

The first non-Indian people to settle in that area had actually arrived in 1833. These were Mark Noble and his wife, who had been living in Chicago, but who purchased land in the region just beyond the two ridges and built a tiny log cabin there. In 1834, Phineas Sherman, with his sons, Phineas Jr., Nicholas, and William, moved into the area from where they had been living on the Des Plaines River (still known as the Aux Plaines at that time), near present day Higgins Road.

In 1835 a steady trickle of settlers began. Sixty-three year old Herman Franzen, a recent immigrant from Germany, did not care much for Chicago, where he was staying; in a letter to a relative he wrote of the "dirty creek named the *checagou*, draining into Lake Michigan its filth," and complained about the general muddiness of the village. In 1835 Franzen took his twenty-five year old daughter, Emma, and his three sons—twenty-two year old John Henry, seventeen-year old Frederick, and twelve-year old Gerhardt—and moved onto eighty acres of land he purchased east of the Des Plaines. The house he and his boys built stood at a point that today would be east of East River Road and just north of Lawrence Avenue.

Twenty-two year old Israel Smith didn't care much for Chicago either. He called it "a perfect mud-hole!" In 1835 he bought a section of land on the first high, dry spot he found on the prairie beyond Chicago; the ridge that would become known as Union Ridge, in what was to become the township of Jefferson. Israel pitched a tent there until he was able to put up a cabin, and he was quickly joined by his brothers; Marcellus, Gustavus,

19

and Waldo, who bought adjoining sections of land all along the ridge, to about where Union Ridge \Cemetery now lies. Later, their father, Henry Smith, also joined them. Because of all these Smiths along the ridge, it quickly became known to the other early settlers as "Smiths Ridge." The land Israel had bought took in what is now Ridgemoor Country Club and the land belonging to St. Rosalie's church and school.

Gardner Brooks also moved from Chicago into the land between the river and the ridges in 1835. And in 1836, a man came into the region whose name is now a part of the Norridge and Harwood Heights area; the man known to the Indians as Che Che Pin Qua, and to the settlers as Alexander Robinson.

When the Indian tribes had left northwestern Illinois and the Chicago area, a tiny handful of Indian men—most of them really only half-Indian—chose to stay. Robinson was one of these. Surprisingly, he had a great deal to do with all the treaties that got the Indians to finally move out of Illinois. When the traders, soldiers, and settlers came back to the Fort Dearborn area after the end of the War of 1812, they found Robinson and his friend Ouilmette farming on the plot of land near the fort's ruins. Because Robinson had helped the Healds and Kinzies after the Fort Dearborn Massacre, he was regarded as friendly and trustworthy, and was quickly accepted as a member of the little community that grew up around the new fort. In fact, on an old document dated 1825, he is listed as one of the only fourteen tax-paying residents of the Chicago community. Thus, when the first U.S. Government Indian Agent arrived to start negotiating treaties for land, he was

Israel Smith, one of the first settlers in the area, as he looked in the late 19th century.

delighted to find Robinson, who spoke both English and Potawatomi, and quickly hired him as an interpreter. So, it was Robinson who generally explained all the treaties to the Potawatomis and other Indians, and who, in most cases, probably convinced them to sign the treaties. In time, the Indians came to look on him as a leader, and apparently made him a kind of honorary chief. Robinson also helped keep the local Indians from causing any trouble during the Winnebago War of 1827 and Blackhawk War of 1832, when there was bloodshed between settlers and Indians in other parts of the state. Because of this, the U.S. Government representatives fixed up Robinson with a private "reservation" of his own on some of the choicest land in the area—about 1,200 acres running from a little south of what is now Irving Park Road to about Foster Avenue, with the Des Plaines River flowing through the middle of it. Most of this area still exists, of course, as the Forest Preserve areas labeled Che Che Pin Qua Woods, Robinson Woods, and Catherine Chevalier Woods (Catherine Chevalier was the name of Robinson's wife at that time). A finger of land sticking out of the main area of Norridge touches a bit of Robinson's former domain—the very bit upon which he is buried, as a matter of fact—and so Norridgers proudly claim him as one of their own. Robinson moved onto his reservation with his wife and four children, but as years went by, a goodly number of relatives, friends, and employees joined them there.

Chief Black Hawk or Ma-Ka-Tai-Me-She-Kia-Kiah, a Saukie leader during the Blackhawk War. Lithograph, 1938.
Photo courtesy Chicago Historical Society.

In 1837 came another settler who bore a name that can still be found in Norridge to this day. It was John Pennoyer, with his twenty-three year old daughter, Susan, and his sons, Stephen, twenty-five, and James, eighteen, and their name is remembered on the Pennoyer School on Cumberland and Foster. They settled on land that lay between what is now East River Road and Cumberland Avenue, north of Lawrence Avenue, and the southwest windows of their home looked toward the long strip of woods that formed much of Alexander Robinson's reservation.

Also in 1837, forty-two year old Francis Tanner came into the area with his wife, Lydia, and their ten-year old son, Henry, while twenty-seven year old Charles Ball settled on a section of prairie that was between what are now Lawrence and Wilson Avenues, through the middle of which Harlem Avenue now runs. In 1838, Herman Rowley and his wife Sarah, with their sons Herman, William, and Aldric, started a farm just north of the present-day Irving Park Road. And there were others.

Thus, by 1839 a number of houses stood in the area, and while they were miles apart from one another, they could easily be seen, one from another, because of the flatness of the land. The little area was a community, although a nameless one.

How did these people live? The men were all farmers who grew crops of mostly oats, corn, and hay on their land. They sold what they could of these crops, in Chicago, and used the rest themselves. Most of them probably had a few cows and hogs. There was plenty of wild game around, and the men often went hunting. From what we know of prairie life in those days, the meals these farmers and their families ate probably consisted mostly of fried

James M. Pennoyer, after whom the Pennoyer School is named, as he appeared in the middle years of his life.

The James Pennoyer family in 1867.

meat, such as pork, ham, and venison (deer), from animals the men killed and cut up themselves, together with a kind of cakelike fresh bread that the women made from ground-up corn mixed with water to form a dough, and baked. In summertime there were wild strawberries and other fruit that children could search for and gather. Such luxuries as salt and coffee had to be bought in Chicago—about a fourteen-mile shopping trip on horseback or in a horse-drawn wagon.

Most of the first houses put up by these people were tiny log cabins with dirt floors. They were heated by wood-burning fireplaces and lighted with candles or lamps that burned whale-oil, which also had to be purchased in Chicago. Most of the women were skilled at making clothing sewn by hand with needle and thread (there were no sewing machines, yet), and most of the men knew how to tan animal hides into leather. If something broke, they fixed it if they could, or made a new one if they could. A family in the area could get by on very little money; one family, the Shermans, managed to live on just fourteen dollars a month (the dollar was, however, worth a good bit more in purchasing power then, than it is now).

The prairie was not really a very healthy place in which to live at this time. Hordes of mosquitoes bred in the water that stood on the flat ground for weeks in the spring and early summer, and they carried a disease some-

Skokie log cabin is typical example of an 1840's home.

what like malaria, which caused shaking chills and fever. It was called "the ague" (pronounced ay-gyoo) or "ager" (ay-gur), by the settlers, and there was no good remedy for it, even though, in 1839, the *Chicago American* newspaper carried an advertisement for "Dr. John Sappington's fever and ague pills." As a matter of fact, doctors of that time did not even know what caused the ague, much less how to cure it. In general, people simply endured it as they endured all the other hardships and privations of log cabin life on the prairie.

The little community quickly began to have special needs that its residents cooperated in taking care of. As early as 1838 a number of the local men gathered at the Pennoyer home to discuss the building of the community's first school. There was, already, a school of sorts, but it was simply held in the Pennoyer home and the teachers were James and Susan Pennoyer, who had been teachers in the east, while the majority of students were Indians from the Robinson reservation and a few local farmers, seeking an education. But with children, such as eleven-year old Henry Tanner, now in the area, it was obvious that a real school was needed. The men came to an agreement that every adult male citizen of the area would contribute the sum of five dollars for materials and would all pitch in to help build a school on land that was being donated by John Pennoyer. This agreement included bachelors as well as the married men, because most of the bachelors expected to get married and have children that would be sent to the school. We can suspect that one of the bachelors who was at the meeting, 25-year old Israel

Union Ridge Cemetery is located on what was once "Smiths Ridge." Many of the early settlers and Civil War soldiers are buried there.

Smith of Smiths Ridge, was already thinking along those lines, and we may speculate that he may have stayed on awhile after the meeting was over, to talk with Miss Susan Pennoyer, and almost certainly often came to visit her from time-to-time afterward—for they were married five years later. The schoolhouse, a small, one-room building standing at what is now the corner of Higgins Road and Canfield Avenue, was finished by the winter of 1838. It became known as the James Pennoyer School, but James apparently never taught in the school that was named after him; Susan Pennoyer was the full-time teacher there until her marriage to Israel Smith. Children who attended the school came from miles around, some of them riding long distances on horseback.

In 1840, the Norridge-Harwood Heights area, as well as the rest of Cook County of course, came close to becoming part of Wisconsin! Politicians of Wisconsin tried to get the United States government to give the fourteen northern counties of Illinois to Wisconsin on the grounds that they had originally belonged to the Wisconsin Territory, which was, to some extent, true. A large number of northern Illinois settlers (although, apparently, none of those in the Harwood Heights-Norridge area) favored becoming part of Wisconsin, and actually held a convention in Rockford, in July of 1840, and "officially" proclaimed the fourteen northern counties as part of Wisconsin's territory. Most Illinoisans were against such a move however, and the government saw no reason to make it. The region remained with Illinois.

Hopeful settlers continued to arrive. In 1840, John Foot came into the area with his wife, Elizabeth, and their baby son, John. Foot was a blacksmith, a welcome addition to a community that depended heavily on horses for pulling ploughs and wagons and for carrying riders from place to place, for horses were often in need of new iron horseshoes, the making of which was a blacksmith's specialty. Also in 1840, William and Mary Dunlap arrived, with their fifteen-year old son, George, and settled on 640 acres that became known as "Dunlap Prairie." In 1843, German immigrants Jacob and Maria Wingert came with their eleven-year old son, John, and in 1844, Jacob and Barbara Kline arrived from Pennsylvania with their family.

It was customary at this time, and for a long time after, for a man to plough a furrow, or ditch, completely around the land he bought. Wood was scarce on the prairie, so there were few if any fences, and the furrows marked the boundaries of each man's farm. They were also a big help in fighting prairie fires, which were frequent during the hot, dry summer months when the sea of prairie grass was so dry and brittle that the smallest spark could turn it into a wall of flame. But such a fire coming to a broad ditch could go no further, and would simply burn itself out.

A great many of the people who came into northern Illinois in the 1830's and '40's were from the New England states, where the form of local government was the "township," or "town" system, in which a county is divided into many townships which each elect their own officials and, to a great extent, govern themselves. The Illinoisans from New England preferred the township system and wanted to have it in their new homeland, so they signed petitions, sent representatives to the state capital, and did everything they could to bring township government to Illinois. They finally succeeded by 1848, when the Illinois state constitution was officially changed to permit any county to switch to township government by taking a vote to see if the majority of the county's citizens wanted to do so. In a vote held in November of 1849, the people of Cook County overwhelmingly elected to switch to the township system, and two of the new townships formed were Leyden and Jefferson, both of which took in parts of the area that would one day include Harwood Heights and Norridge.

By this time, a number of old Indian trails had become well-traveled roads, and some new roads, made by the settlers, were running through the area. Some of these are now streets that run through Harwood Heights and Norridge and nearby areas, although the names are now generally different. A north-south stagecoach trail had been designated as the dividing line between the two new townships, Leyden and Jefferson, and became known as Township Line Road. Today, it is Harlem Avenue. A dirt road that ran between the land owned by Israel and Marcellus Smith was known as Smiths Road. It is now Gunnison Street. Running along parallel to the Des Plaines River was a thoroughfare with the descriptive name of Skunk Road. Now we call it Cumberland Avenue. A road that crossed the river at a point where the Brooks Tavern stood was known as Brooks Road, and apparently this is the present East River Road. And a thoroughfare known as the Plank Road is now Irving Park Road. It was originally called Plank Road because it was actually formed of wooden planks set in a long row. It was built in 1850 by the Plank Road Company, which put up a sawmill just about where Irving Park Road now crosses the Des Plaines River, to saw planks for the road, using wood from the trees around the river. There were a good many such plank roads throughout northern Illinois by the late 1840's, because the rains that fell in spring and autumn turned the prairie into mud, and ordinary dirt roads often became quagmires in which horses would sometimes actually sink up to their bellies and become unable to move. Plank roads were an attempt to create roads that could be used all year around. However, they apparently did not work too well, as the planks often warped and rotted, making the road dangerous—a horse could easily break a leg.

The planks were mostly all gone by the end of the 1850's, but for a long time, Irving Park Road continued to be known as the Old Plank Road.

In 1851, officials of the new Leyden Township apparently felt that a new school was needed in the area, for they purchased a portion of land at what is now Irving Park Road and Ozanam Avenue from Herman Rowley for the sum of five dollars, which was a very healthy sum at that time. The one-room schoolhouse built there was called Leyden Township School Number Four, and was mainly attended by children living south of Old Plank Road. Also in 1851, the Cook County government bought 100 acres of land in the area that now lies between Irving Park Road and Forest Preserve Drive, just east of Harlem Avenue. The land was intended to be used for a "poor farm," a place where all the county's homeless, jobless, hopeless widows, orplans, handicapped people and elderly people could be sent to stay when they had nowhere else to turn. There, they would be fed, clothed, and sheltered in return for whatever work they could do on the farm to help pay for their keep. This was the 19th century version of welfare. At first, the poor farm was known simply as "Jefferson," because it was located near the township of Jefferson. A large brick building, which was to serve as the "poorhouse," was finished in 1855, along with a smaller building which was intended as a place to keep people that the county officials decided were

The Old Leyden Indian Agency house built approximately 1840. It stood near the 8100 block of Lawrence Ave.   *Photo courtesy Leyden Historical Research, Inc.*

28

"crazy"—in tiny, jail-like cells that were seven by eight feet in area, with barred doors!

More people came into the area in the 1850's. C.P. Grant and his wife, Martha, settled on 31 acres north of what is now Lawrence Avenue, between Canfield and Harlem, in 1853. Melchior Miller settled in what is now the Norridge area that same year.

By the end of the 1850's the area no longer had the look of a frontier settlement. Much of the prairie had been turned into farmland and few if any log cabins were left; they had mostly been replaced by typical 19th century American farmhouses of wooden siding, generally whitewashed or painted pale gray, with black or dark-brown wood-shingled roofs. There were well-defined dirt roads serving the area, and two schools. The little community that would someday become Norridge and Harwood Heights was now a quarter of a century old.

And over that community, as over every other part of the United States, a dark cloud was gathering.

CHAPTER 3

WAR, CATASTROPHE, AND LOCAL POLITICS: 1861-1899

WAR, CATASTROPHE, AND LOCAL POLITICS: 1861-1899

WITH the dawning of 1860, the first year of a new decade, the people living in the area of the two ridges surely knew, as did most other Americans, that the United States was on the verge of a civil war. Throughout the late 1850's there had already been actual warfare between pro-slavery and anti-slavery factions in the territory of Kansas, and in 1859 John Brown had made his unsuccessful raid on Harper's Ferry, Virginia, to seize weapons from a federal arsenal and start a slave uprising in the South. In May of 1860, Abraham Lincoln was nominated for the presidency by the Republican party, in Chicago, and prominent Southerners were calling for the Southern slavery states to withdraw from the union if he was elected. In some parts of Illinois there were people who favored the Southern cause, but it is safe to say that the people of the two ridges were solidly against slavery. It is a matter of record, for example, that Israel Smith, one of the area's leading citizens, was a staunch supporter of the Abolitionist, or anti-slavery movement, and Jessie Ball went to Kansas for a time, in 1856, to help the anti-slavery people there work toward bringing Kansas into the union as a free state, in which slavery would not be permitted.

In December, South Carolina withdrew from the union, and by March of 1861 six more Southern states had also seceded. On April 12, Southern troops attacked the U.S. fortress of Fort Sumter, in Charleston (South Carolina) Harbor, and the American Civil War had begun. In North and South, a call for volunteer soldiers went out.

The area of the two ridges seems to have given more than its share to the Northern cause. Of course, to an eighteen or nineteen-year old boy brought up on a farm at that time, doing the same things day in and day out, and with nothing much to look forward to but more of the same, going to war seemed like a glorious adventure. The idea of putting on a colorful uniform, going off to fight against a rebellious enemy that was seeking to destroy your country's government, and coming back a hero to be admired by your elders—as well as all the pretty young girls in the area—was tremendously exciting when compared to a future of pulling onions and mowing hay. The young men of the area, and a number of older ones as well, flocked to enlist.

Early in 1861, 34-year old Henry Tanner enlisted in Company B of the McClellan Dragoons, a cavalry unit organized in Chicago and named in honor of the general who was then commanding the Union Army. Henry's intentions were good, but he never got to face the enemy—during his period of training he was thrown from a horse and so badly injured that he spent four and a half months in the hospital and was then given an honorable discharge and sent home.

Twenty-one year old John Foot, son of the local blacksmith, also enlisted in Company B of the McClellan Dragoons early in 1861. We can guess that he and Tanner may have talked it over beforehand and went to join up together. But Foot did get to face the enemy. He fought in the Battle of Hannover Court House, early in the war, and then was involved in the Seven Days Battles that took place outside Richmond, Virginia, from June 25 to July 1, 1862. Wounded there, at the Battle of White Oak Swamp, he was given a disability discharge and returned home, no doubt to the admiration of his elders and numerous pretty girls, one of whom he married in 1865.

Late in the war another Tanner—Ledore Tanner—also offered himself to the Northern cause. He became a member of Company I of the 88th Illinois Infantry. He, too, made it back home.

In 1863, Solomon Burhans, a 37-year old farmer, tried to raise a volunteer company with himself as an officer, as was often done at that time. However, the army rejected Burhans because of physical disabilities, so his dream of serving was never realized.

Actually, of course, Burhans, Foot, and the Tanners and their families were lucky, because these men had survived the war. There were others of the two ridges area who were not so lucky. Jessie and Drusilla Ball's son, Zebina, joined the Union Army in 1861, and on May 4, 1862, he was killed during the Union advance against Corinth, Mississippi. He was nineteen years old. A year later, the Ball's other son, Arza, also went into the Union Army. On May 27, 1864, at the Battle of New Hope Church, in Georgia, he was wounded, and died two days later—also at the age of nineteen years.

The Ball's neighbors, Allen and Harriet Hemingway, who had come into the area in 1854 and began farming near what is now Harlem Avenue and Higgins Road, also lost two sons in the war between the states. For these two families, those were bitter years.

On April 9, 1865, General Robert E. Lee surrendered to U.S. Grant and the Civil War was over. But the gladness over the war's end, and the celebrations that must have been held in the Jefferson-Leyden area, as elsewhere in the North, were quickly ended by the shocking news, five days later, that President Lincoln had been assassinated. This may have meant a bit more to people of Illinois communities than to other parts of the nation, for Abe Lincoln was an Illinoisan, and there were people in the area of the two ridges, as elsewhere in Illinois, who had known him. Alexander Robinson—Che Che Pin Qua—for example, had once held a long conversation with Lincoln involving a legal matter which Lincoln, then a young lawyer, was handling. So, while there were shock and anger throughout most of the Northern states, there was surely some sincere sadness in the two ridges area and other Illinois communities.

But in time, the worry and excitement of the war and the anger and sadness of the assassination faded into memory, and even for those men who had experienced the war first-hand, and those families that had felt the bitter loss of loved ones, life slipped into old, familiar day-to-day patterns.

But not entirely. Some new ideas were stirring in the region of the two ridges. During the last half of the 1860's, people began to grow more and more discontented over the way their tax money was being used by the local government; particularly the government of Jefferson Township. Like everyone else in the township, they paid taxes for the upkeep of the roads and streets in their area, but while the roads and streets in every other part of Jefferson Township were being kept in good condition, or so it seemed, those in the two ridges area were in such bad shape they could hardly be used. Protests to the township didn't do a bit of good, either. And so, the people of the area had grown good and angry—they were paying their taxes and not getting a thing in return!

It was apparently George Dunlap, who had come into the region as a teen-ager in 1840, with his parents, and was now a successful businessman of 44, who came up with the idea of forming a *new* township in the area. If a new township could be formed, the people within it would pay taxes for their roads to *it*, instead of to Jefferson Township, and could see to it that they got what they needed. It seemed like a good way of getting even with the Jefferson Township politicians who had been ignoring them, and most people thought Dunlap's idea was great.

There was only one problem. To have a township, there had to be a town, and there were only scattered farmhouses in the area. But Dunlap had the answer to that—he would simply put a town together! In 1869 he built a two-story frame house at what would later be the corner of Norwood Court and Circle Avenue. Two other houses quickly went up close by, built by other residents of the area. Almost as if to help out, the Chicago and North-western Railroad built a station nearby (now the Norwood Park station, of course). A couple of businessmen took a chance and put up a store. Another group of businessmen built a hotel.

So, there was the town—mighty small, but undeniably real. Of course, it needed a name. One of the famous "personalities" of that time was a Presbyterian preacher by the name of Henry Ward Beecher, and in 1867 Beecher had written a novel entitled *Norwood: A Tale of Village Life in New England*, which became a sort of best seller. Dunlap and some of his neighbors had read the book and were obviously charmed by the name Beecher had invented for the village in the tale, because that was the name they chose for their new town. They quickly discovered a problem, however, for it seemed there was a Norwood Post Office in another part of the Chicagoland area then, and there might be confusion over the delivery of mail. But they solved the problem by simply adding the word "Park" to the name of their new community. Thus, Norwood Park was conceived.

About this time, in 1870, a large brick building began to go up on the grounds of the county poor farm and insane asylum on Old Plank (Irving Park) Road. It was a new modern hospital with rooms and accomodations

James Giles, after whom the Giles School is named, as he appeared in 1937. *Photo courtesy Giles School.*

for 300 patients. By now there was a much more humane attitude toward people suffering from mental problems, and the hospital was made as roomy, clean, light and airy as possible, and a staff of younger, better-trained doctors was put in charge. The poor farm and hospital area was now generally known as "Dunning," in honor of Andrew Dunning who had come into the region in 1865 and had donated land for a railroad line to make travel easier between the hospital and the city of Chicago.

1870 also saw the coming of a new family of settlers whose name has remained in Norridge and Harwood Heights to this day. The Giles family, including seven children, one of which was seven-year old James Giles, came straight from England and settled near Irving Park Road, later moving to a point about where the Baptist Home now is, at Lawrence and Canfield Avenues.

Throughout 1870 and 1871, George Dunlap continued his efforts to bring the new township of Norwood Park into being. But now, something occurred which, for a time at least, took everyone's thoughts away from local politics. Farmers of the area, leaving their houses to start the day's chores in the still-dark, early-morning hours of October 9, 1871, saw an eastern sky that glowed bright red and was filled with billowing smoke. The city of Chicago was being consumed by a gigantic raging fire!

The Great Chicago Fire started on the evening of October 8 and burned for twenty-four hours, wiping out a large portion of the city. It swept through an area roughly between Harrison Street and Fullerton Avenue, west from the lake shore to Halsted Street and the south branch of the river. In that area it destroyed about 15,000 homes and 2,500 other buildings, including the county courthouse and waterworks. Three hundred people were killed and some 90,000 left homeless by the time it finally burned itself out. An area of the "Dunning" grounds was used as a common burial ground for unidentified victims of the fire.

Unfortunately, we have no records of how people of the future Norridge-Harwood Heights area were affected by the fire. Some of them must have had friends or relatives in Chicago, and were probably badly worried about their safety. Some area residents, such as Israel Smith, had businesses in the city, and so may have suffered severe losses of money or property. We know that after 1871 Israel Smith no longer had a business in Chicago, but had returned to full-time farming, and this may have been because his Chicago business, a store, was destroyed. We can guess that some of the other people of this area were also hurt by the fire, either personally or financially, and that most of them must have regarded it as a dreadful catastrophe.

But for at least one resident, the burning-to-the-ground of much of Chicago was *not* a catastrophe. Che Che Pin Qua—Alexander Robinson—went to look at the ruins, and as he stood by the Lake Street bridge and gazed out over the blackened, smoldering litter of ashes, tumbled bricks, and melted metal that was all that was left of the skyline, he suddenly let out an exultant whoop and loudly exclaimed that now he could again see the prairie from this place, as he had been able to do when he was a young man. Clearly, *he* regarded the elimination of all those buildings, that had been blotting out the natural world, as a blessing!

Robinson was extremely old by this time, and in spring of the next year, 1872, he died. Because he was a truly historical figure, closely connected with the birth of Chicago, there was considerable interest in him. On May 14, 1872, the *Chicago Tribune* published a long obituary headed, "DEATH OF A POTAWATOMI CHIEF NEAR CHICAGO," recounting many of the legends that had grown up around Robinson—such as that he had died at the age of 104, which is doubtful.

Alexander Robinson is buried, together with members of his family, on a plot of Forest Preserve ground on the northwest corner of East River Road and Lawrence Avenue, which was once in the heart of his reservation. A brown-and-yellow signboard informs passers-by that this is the site of the Robinson Family Burial Ground. Anyone seeking to visit the grave passes through an opening in a rustic wooden fence, takes a very brief, winding walk through a grove of trees, and comes to a tiny clearing in the center of which sits a huge chunk of reddish rock, upon which are carved the words:

> *Alexander Robinson*
> *Chee Chee Pin Quay**
> *Chief of the Potowatami, Chippewa, and Ottawa Indians*
> *Who died April 27, 1872*
> *Catherine (Chevalier) his wife*
> *Who died August 7, 1860*
> *And other members of their family*
> *Are buried on this spot*
> *Part of the reservation granted him*
> *By the treaty of Prairie du Chien*
> *July 29, 1829*
> *In gratitude for his aid to the family*
> *of John Kinzie, and to Capt. and Mrs. Heald*
> *At the time of the Fort Dearborn Massacre*

There are rustic wooden benches for anyone who wishes to sit and meditate. It is a very pleasant and suitable spot; even though traffic is whizzing by on two sides less than fifty yards away, the cars are hidden by trees. It

*The name is spelled in different ways on various historical markers and in historical records.

The original gravestones of **Alexander Robinson and his wife, Catherine Chevalier, were replaced many years later by the present grave marker shown below.**

Photo courtesy Chicago Historical Society.

ALEXANDER ROBINSON

(CHEE-CHEE-PIN-QUAY)
CHIEF OF THE POTAWATOMI, CHIPPEWA AND OTTAWA INDIANS
WHO DIED APRIL 22, 1872
CATHERINE (CHEVALIER) HIS WIFE
WHO DIED AUGUST 7, 1860
AND OTHER MEMBERS OF THEIR FAMILY
ARE BURIED ON THIS SPOT —
PART OF THE RESERVATION GRANTED HIM
BY THE TREATY OF PRAIRIE DU CHIEN
JULY 29, 1829
IN GRATITUDE FOR HIS AID TO THE FAMILY
OF JOHN KINZIE AND TO CAPT. AND MRS. HEALD
AT THE TIME OF THE FORT DEARBORN MASSACRE

Marker located on forest preserve land at the site of the Robinson family burial ground.

is a place of real historical significance for Norridge and Harwood Heights; something such as few other comparable communities can boast. However, it must be told that, for a number of decades at least, it has been an item of folklore among the children of Harwood Heights and Norridge that every

Halloween night, the ghost of Che Che Pin Qua comes out and takes a look around!

With the dawning of 1873, everything was finally ready for the move to have the new town of Norwood Park officially recognized so that the new township could come into existence. The politicians of Jefferson Park Township, and to a lesser extent those of Leyden Township, were not at all happy about this, for the new township would be carved out of portions of their areas, and they would lose tax money as a result. They referred to Norwood Park as "the pretended town of Norwood Park," and tried to get the county and state officials to refuse to recognize it.

But they were unsuccessful. There were thirty voters in the proposed Norwood Park area, and twenty of them had signed George Dunlap's petition to create the new township. That was sufficient. The county board accepted the petition and recognized the town, officially creating the new township of Norwood Park out of adjoining sections of Jefferson Park and Leyden Townships.

On April 1st, the voters of Norwood Park Township elected their first

The Horton farmhouse in 1900 (above) once stood on the site of Norridge Theater, W. Bell & Co., Egghead and Sound Warehouse (below).

Walter D. Phillips, an area farmer of the 1890s.

government. A good many of the "old-time" early settlers, or members of their families, became township officials. Stephen Pennoyer was elected Supervisor; Jessie Ball was Assessor; Frederick Kline, Collector; Civil War veteran John Foot, a Justice of the Peace; Israel Smith, a Highway Commissioner. There was some wrangling between this new government and the government officials of Jefferson Park Township over some of the tax money that had already been collected, but this was straightened out. The new township was off and running.

There were a great many children in the area now, and more schools were needed. In 1875 farmer Charles Ball donated an acre of land for the schoolground, and other farmers donated materials and their labor to build a one-room schoolhouse just about where Union Ridge School now stands. The school opened in 1876, and at first it was apparently known as "Smiths Schoolhouse," possibly because it was near the dirt road still known as Smiths Road (now Gunnison Street), or perhaps because the first teacher was Miss Kittie Smith, daughter of old-time settler Israel Smith. At any rate, fifteen children, ranging from first-graders to eighth-graders, attended it, making their way along Smith's Road or coming up a cinder path that would one day be Oak Park Avenue, and often cutting through fields of corn and onions, for there were not, of course, any sidewalks in the area. In winter, the school was heated by a single potbellied, coal-burning, iron stove; in summer, thirsty children would have to go to the nearest farmhouse, the Sass home, to get a drink of water from the outdoor pump.

Two years later, several miles to the southwest, farmer Lawrence Guthier sold a strip of his property to the local school directors. It adjoined property

Union Ridge School in 1876. *Photo courtesy Union Ridge School.*

that had been bought for school purposes some twenty-seven years earlier, and now a new three-room schoolhouse was built on the land. Three teachers were hired, one for each room, and 127 children, from first to eighth grade, were soon attending classes. This school stood just about where the Village Florist shop now stands (c. 1988) on Irving Park near Ozanam, and for some reason—possibly because it was on land that had been annexed, or taken over, from Leyden Township—it became known as The Annex, a name that was to stick for over seventy years.

All this time, the City of Chicago was creeping ever closer. In the year Norwood Park came into being, the western boundary of the city was at Crawford Avenue. In 1889, Jefferson Park, which by then was well-crowded with houses and business and factory buildings, was added on as part of Chicago, and the westernmost boundary was at Harlem Avenue, from North Avenue to Lawrence Avenue. Four years later, in 1893, the town of Norwood Park, with its railroad station, hotel, stores, homes, and a portion of the surrounding farmland, also joined the city.

But the little area of Norwood Park Township that was to become Harwood Heights and Norridge was left outside. It was still all "country"; a cluster of farms and scattered farmhouses, generally a half-mile or so apart from one another, with a few dirt roads and cinder paths running here and there, and a couple of little country schools. It had nothing that the city wanted, and apparently, it did not particularly want the city.

It had continued to gain people. In 1873, William Phillips and his wife Mary Ann, from England, bought ten acres of land just north of Irving Park Road, covering part of what is now Acacia Park Cemetery. The road that ran north along the edge of Phillips' property became known as Phillips

Street (it is now Ozanam Avenue). In 1884, Frederick Harris bought farmland on Lawrence Avenue near Phillips Street. In the 1890's, Gerhard, John, and Peter van Bergen all bought farms in the area.

Acacia Park Cemetery.

The James Pennoyer School, and the children of the area, in 1893.

Photo courtesy Pennoyer School.

43

The last ten years of the nineteenth century were not particularly good ones for the nation. In 1893 there was a "Panic," or depression, in which more than 500 banks closed, 16,000 businesses failed, and hundreds of thousands of people were thrown out of work by the end of the year. Farmers in the midwest were badly hurt by falling prices for their crops, and we can suspect that times were bad for most of the farmers of the future Norridge-Harwood Heights area, too. However, most of them seem to have weathered the storm, and by 1898, things were pretty well back to normal again. The 1800's came to an end, and the little scattering of farms that would one day be Norridge and Harwood Heights slipped quietly into the twentieth century.

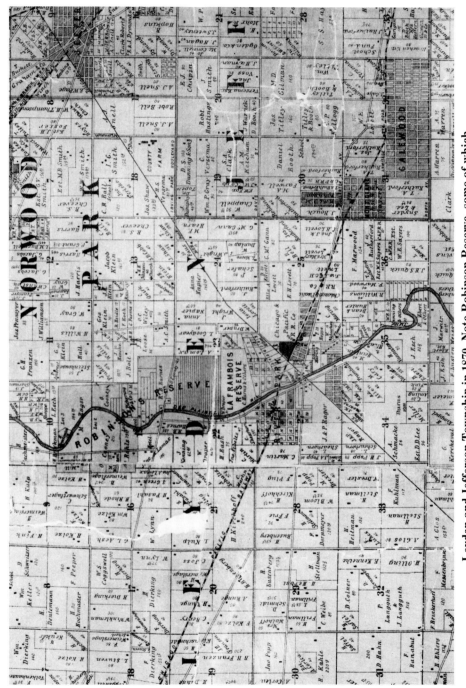

Leyden and Jefferson Township in 1870. Note Robinson Reserve, some of which is now part of Cook County Forest Preserve System. Also County Farm which was later called Dunning.

CHAPTER 4

FROM FARM COMMUNITY TO GROWING SUBURB: 1900-1945

FROM FARM COMMUNITY TO GROWING SUBURB: 1900-1945

A SURPRISING number of the original settlers of the area were still alive at the beginning of the twentieth century, and still living in or near the little southwest corner section of Norwood Park Township. One of these was one of the very first settlers, Israel Smith, who had been residing on his farm on Union Ridge for sixty-five years, since 1835. Smith died in 1904, at the age of eighty-eight.

Another "old timer" was the Civil War veteran John Foot, who had come into the area as a baby with his parents in 1840. Foot died in 1908, at age sixty-eight. Gerhard Franzen, who had been twelve years old in 1835 when his parents came into the two-ridges region, also died in 1908, at the age of eighty-five. He had been living a short distance outside Norwood Park Township, on the farm he had started in 1847. Part of this farm is now part of O'Hare Airport; it was the first land to be bought for the airport, in 1943.

Ledore Tanner, another Civil War veteran, who had been born in the area in 1846 and lived in it all his life, also died in 1908. George Kline, a nine-year old when his parents came in 1844, died in 1911, and his brother Frederick, a seven-year old in 1844, died in 1914. And so, the last of the pioneer settlers of the area were gone. These were the people who could remember what the prairie had looked like before it had all been turned into farmland, and who had lived in log cabins or even in tents for a time. For them, Illinois had been the western frontier. By the beginning of the twentieth century it was part of the heartland of the United States—a typical midwestern farm community.

For the area was still almost entirely farmland. Main roads such as Irving Park Road and Canfield Road, and a few streets such as Phillips Street

**Bringing hay to market in the Norwood Park Township
area during the first quarter of the 20th Century.**

Road graders at Harlem and Lawrence Avenues, early in the 20th Century.

(Ozanam), ran through parts of it, but the north-and-south running "O"
streets that now characterize so much of Norridge and Harwood Heights,
were still mostly under farmland, such as the Drewes family farm which
lay between what is now Irving Park Road and Lawrence Avenue, and
through the very center of which Oriole Avenue would one day run.

The existing roads and streets were still unpaved at the beginning of the
twentieth century, and the houses sitting back off the roads were similar
to old houses that can still be seen in rural parts of Illinois, Iowa, and
Missouri—white or pale gray two-story wooden frame houses with lacy
curtains in every window, narrow porches with flights of wooden steps

50

The John Sell farmhouse.

leading up to them, and sloping, shingled roofs. Few if any of these houses had indoor plumbing, so most of them had an iron pump sticking up out of the ground nearby, from which one could pump up well water by pushing a long, creaking iron handle up and down. It always took a couple of pushes before the water would come flowing out of the nozzle, and water would continue to flow for a moment or two after the pushing was stopped. There were no toilet facilities in any of those houses either, so out behind each one stood what was known as an "outhouse," "backhouse," or, "privy"; a sort of small wooden shed with a door that generally had a small half-moon shaped opening in it, for light and ventilation. Within the outhouse was a wide, smooth board, set horizontally at about chairseat level, with two or more different-sized circular holes cut in it. Beneath the board, under the floor of the outhouse, was a pit called a cess-pool.

The insides of the houses were not much different from the houses of forty or fifty years earlier. They were lighted with gas-burning or kerosene-burning lamps, much like those used by campers today. Food was cooked on wood-burning or coal-burning stoves, and coal-burning stoves were generally used to heat the house in wintertime. It wasn't until 1913 that wires carrying electricity were brought into the area, and not until 1916 that gas pipes were extended from the city, and sewers were installed. Gradually, such things as electric lights and gas stoves came into the farmhouses.

In 1903 a congregation was formed for the area's first permanent church, and a year later a building was put up on land that had been a farmer's onion field, at what is now 5650 Canfield Road in Chicago. This was the St. Paul Evangelical Lutheran Church, Missouri Synod, and the first pastor was the Rev. August H. Lange. For the first nineteen years of the church's

The Frederick Franzen homestead.

The John van Bergen farm.

existence, services were held entirely in the German language, indicating that the area must have abounded in people of German origin.

In 1908, an organization calling itself the Irving Golf Club bought the entire Israel Smith farm on Union Ridge, and turned it into a country club with a nine-hole golf course. What had been Israel Smith's home, a two-story red brick building, was used as the clubhouse, and some of the members, most of whom were fairly wealthy, would park their Stanley Steamer automobiles under the cherry trees in what had been Smith's cherry orchard. A special horse-drawn carriage bus would bring other members from the train stations at Norwood Park and Jefferson Park.

From December of 1910 to June of 1912, the people working on the poor farm at Dunning were gradually all moved to Oak Forest Hospital, in another

The Irving Golf Club, now the Ridgemoor Country Club, in the early 1900s.
Photo courtesy Ridgemoor Country Club.

part of the county, and only the mental patients were left at the institution. On June 29, 1912, the county officially sold Dunning to the state of Illinois for the traditional legal sum of one dollar. The state renamed the place the Chicago State Hospital, but it continued to be known, locally and throughout the Chicagoland area, as Dunning.

Also in 1912, the St. Paul Evangelical Lutheran Church opened a parochial school for the children of its congregation. Inasmuch as this school, although now in its third building, still stands where it was begun, it is actually the second-oldest school in the area, after Union Ridge School.

In 1914, the country club on Union Ridge officially became Ridgemoor

**Many of the Dunning buildings, dating to the early part
of the 20th Century, were still standing in the late 1970s.**

Country Club. That same year, war broke out in Europe; the war we now
call World War One. In 1915, the year that James Giles built a new farmhouse
at Harlem and Montrose Avenues, trenches wound through northern France
and men were dying by the tens of thousands. By 1917 the United States
had been drawn into the war. About 2,800,000 men between the ages of 21
and 30 were drafted into the U.S. armed forces; some two million more
voluntarily enlisted, and a little more than two million were sent "overseas"
to France.

The Norridge-Harwood Heights area does not seem to have suffered losses from World War One as it did from the Civil War. Ralph Harris, of the area's Harris family, served in the army, but returned home safely and lived to a good age. In 1918, Ridgemoor Country Club held a special golf tournament to raise funds for the Red Cross, and most local farmers probably bought some of the Liberty Bonds that were being sold to help the war effort, but aside from such things, the community was apparently untouched. The war ended in late 1918.

The nation now entered a time of prosperity. In the early 1920's the part of Irving Park Road that ran through the southwest corner of Norwood Park Township was paved, as were Harlem and Narragansett Avenues. A small area just off Irving Park Road, running east from Ozanam, was subdivided by a building company, given the proud name of John Kinzie Estates, and a number of houses were built on it. A small residential community began to grow. However, there weren't enough people in the area to make it worthwhile for the Chicago streetcar company to extend its lines to them; the streetcar track that ran on Irving Park Road through Chicago ended at Narragansett, near Dunning, a good ten blocks from the new little community.

In 1922, Mr. Street Lightfoot, a businessman specializing in the formation of cemeteries, purchased the Phillips farm which ran north from Irving Park Road to Montrose and west from Ozanam Avenue to what is now Thatcher Road. On this land was created the Acacia Park Cemetery, originally a cemetery for members of the Masonic order.

The clubhouse of the Ridgemoor Country Club in 1917.
Photo courtesy Ridgemoor Country Club.

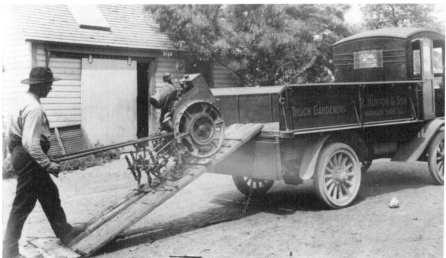

Truck farming on the Horton farm in the early 1920s.

By now, a model-T Ford had replaced the horse-drawn bus that brought members to the Ridgemoor Country Club during the war. It would meet the 5:45 train from Chicago at the Jefferson Park station and drive members to Ridgemoor for dinner. One of the members now was W. A. Wieboldt, founder of the Wieboldt department store chain. From 1925 to 1929 Ridgemoor held an annual golf tournament that attracted top players from all over the country; such famous names as Walter Hagan, Tommy Armour, and Gene Sarazan, which are now all in the record books.

It was in the early 1920's that James Giles decided to relocate to another part of the area. He considered building a new home, but finally decided it

A tractor on the W. Phillips farm in the 1920s.

would be far cheaper to simply move the house he already had, at Harlem and Montrose, so it was taken off its foundation and carried by truck to its new location at Lawrence and Overhill, where it was to stand for the next sixty some years.

In the twenties, nearly all the farmers of the area were doing what is known as truck farming; growing crops that could be loaded into a truck and taken into the city for sale. The main crops were corn, squash, carrots, onions, tomatoes, parsnips and horseradish. Farmwork was still mainly done by hand and was often back-breakingly hard. For example, workers tending a horseradish crop had to crawl along the ground, digging up the plants and pulling off the root tendrils, then sticking the plants carefully back into the earth. To harvest squash, workers trudged among the vines, hacking off the ripe yellow vegetables with big, machete-like knives, then forming a "bucket brigade" to toss the squashes from one worker to another to be piled into a heap at the edge of the field, for pickup. Most of the farmers hired people to come from the city and do these jobs. Pay was generally one dollar a day, plus lunch and dinner. The farmers would load their trucks with produce and drive in to the markets on South Water Street or Randolph Street, in Chicago, to sell what they could to the wholesale warehouses there.

During the 1920's there was a great deal of activity involving schools. In 1922, the third school named after James Monroe Pennoyer was built at the corner of Canfield Avenue and Higgins Road, just where the very first one had stood. In 1924, another school district was merged with Union Ridge

**James Monroe Pennoyer School, built 1922 at the
corner of Canfield Avenue and Higgins Road.**

District 86, and the enrollment at Union Ridge School jumped from 33 to 153. A two-room building was hastily put up next to the old Union Ridge School building, and three new teachers were hired. In 1927, a new building housing 125 students was put up on the Annex property, but it was obvious this wouldn't be sufficient for very long, and the District 80 schoolboard bought five acres of land at what is now Cullom and Oriole, from farmer John Sass, for a new school building. The building was finished in 1928 and was named the James Giles School, in honor of the man who had come into the community in 1870, as an eight-year old, and had spent the rest of his life in the community, becoming Township Supervisor and President of the Board of Education, among other things. It was an eight-room school with an assembly hall.

Farmland surrounded the school. A field of squash lay just behind it, to the east, and the children were warned not to take short-cuts through this, on their way to and from the school building. The farmer who owned this field had hired a number of migrant Jamaican farmworkers to help harvest his crops, and they lived right on his land, in a cluster of tiny shacks, their children attending the Giles school along with the local children.

One other event involving a school during this time was much less pleasant. In September of 1929 a fire destroyed the 53-year old one-room Union Ridge School building. A new, four-room brick building was quickly put up in its place.

There were now enough people in the area so that there was a distinct need for more churches. In June of 1928 the Acacia Community Presbyterian

The Giles School Annex class of 1925-26. The Annex, in the background, stood at what is now the northwest corner of Ozanam Avenue and Irving Park Road.
Photo courtesy Giles School.

Church was formed, holding services in a temporary building on Ozanam Avenue. The pastor was the Reverend George Cleaver. That same year, the United Lutheran Church of Illinois Synod sent a student minister, A. Roy Addy, into the area and he began a Mission Church with 36 members in a rented store on the corner of Irving Park and Overhill. When United Lutheran Church officials learned that the Episcopal Church of Norwood Park building was for sale for three hundred dollars, they bought it, purchased some land on the northeast corner of Oriole and Cullom, across from the Giles school, and had the entire building moved across the fields from its site to the new property. A. Roy Addy was ordained a full-fledged minister, and the Acacia Park Lutheran Church came into being.

By this time, some of the non-farmers living in the tiny residential area building up north of Irving Park Road were beginning to suffer from the problems that would plague them for the next twenty or so years. Living "out in the sticks," as they did, they had none of the ordinary conveniences that citizens of towns and cities took for granted—such things as sidewalks, paved streets, streetlights, and police and fire protection. Of course, people in towns and cities, which are "incorporated areas," pay taxes for such things, whereas people of "unincorporated areas" outside towns and cities do not, and therefore do not have them. A move began to grow among the non-farmers to try to have the area annexed, or joined to, Chicago. If the area were to become part of the city, the city government would take care of all its needs and simply levy taxes on it.

But the farmers of the area were against annexation. They had no need of paved streets, sidewalks, or street lighting, and weren't willing to pay taxes for such things. As long as they had good main roads such as Irving Park Road and Harlem Avenue, on which to get their produce into the city, and for which they paid taxes to the county, they were perfectly satisfied. They had more power than the handful of homeowners, so the idea of annexation was never allowed to get anywhere, and the homeowners stopped pushing for it.

Actually, the homeowners may have stopped pushing for annexation simply because they thought it was going to happen anyway. In the late 1920's there was a strong belief that a tremendous building-boom was going to take place on the outskirts of Chicago, and that houses would soon be springing up in the areas of farmland. Because of this, the county put some sidewalks into the little southwest corner section of Norwood Park Township, running straight through miles of farmland. These were a joy to children of the area, because they provided long, smooth, straight places on which to go roller skating. They were also a kind of symbolic promise to the homeowners that the area was soon to be built-up and they would get the improvements and services they wanted.

However, the expected building boom never happened. On October 24, 1929—a day that became known as Black Thursday—the price of stocks (shares of business firms, mines, power companies, etc.) took a sudden drastic drop. During the next few days, stocks that had been worth a great deal of money became almost worthless, and banks and businesses that had invested in large amounts of stocks lost all the money they had invested, and had to close. Millions of people lost all their savings, millions of people were suddenly thrown out of work. The time of the Great Depression had come, and there weren't going to be any "building booms" for a good many years.

During the Depression there were hard times in the area that was to become Norridge and Harwood Heights, as there were hard times most everywhere. The truck farmers not only had to worry about their normal problems, such as not enough rain or too much rain; now they also had to worry about the way prices were dropping. Sometimes they couldn't get any more than twelve cents for seventy-two good ears of sweet corn, from the wholesalers in Chicago. To bolster their sagging incomes, many farmers put up roadside stands, and during summer and fall sold produce cheaply to passing motorists and people who came out from the city to take advantage

The Episcopal Church of Norwood Park (above) was moved from its location and remodeled to become the Acacia Park Lutheran Church in 1929.

of the low prices. In the weeks before July fourth, many farmers would rent their stands to sellers of fireworks, which were then legal in Illinois.

Many of the homeowners of the area had problems, too, for a lot of them had lost their jobs and couldn't find new ones. But people pulled together and kept things going as best they could. The James Giles School became a kind of center for community fund-raising activities. Women of the PTA crocheted home-made lace to raise the money needed for coal to heat the school, shades for classroom windows, and other such things. Various kinds of community events were held in the school basement.

Entertainment during those days was cheap and simple. Groups of neighbors might occasionally chip in and go for a "hayride" at night, on the pitch-black country roads, in a hay-packed farm wagon drawn by clip-clopping horses, with a single lantern swinging from the back of the wagon, to alert any automobile drivers that might be using the lonely roads at night. Community dances were sometimes held at a two-story building on Oketo, the music being supplied by a pianist who was paid with the change collected from the dancers when a hat was passed among them. For young people, there were long night walks on the stretches of sidewalk, with the thick darkness broken only by a few distant twinkling lights on Irving Park Road. There were a few buildings known as "roadhouses" there, which were basically just restaurants with live entertainment and dancing, and there were two buildings that housed gambling casinos (one reputed to have connections with the famous Chicago gangster, Al Capone) but few, if any, of the people of the region could afford to, or cared to, go to these places. Most of the patrons were Chicago people who hadn't been badly hurt by the Depression.

There were also a number of milk stores on Irving Park Road and Harlem Avenue at this time. Milk was not sold in cartons or even in bottles at these places; people brought in their own pitchers or glass jars and had them filled, paying for whatever the amount of milk came to. Many people, in those days, had their milk delivered in bottles, by a "milkman" who came in a horse-drawn wagon or a truck, but this was more expensive than buying from a milk store.

Many people came to live in the area during the Depression, because the living was a little cheaper. Inasmuch as it was an unincorporated area there were fewer taxes to pay. A sadly large number of homes had been abandoned because their owners had been unable to keep up the mortgage payments on them, so a good house could often be bought for as little as $2,500.00. Among the families that came into the pre-Norridge area during Depression times was the Leigh family, with a teen-age boy named John, who was destined to leave his name in the community to the present day.

Kandler's Dairy (William Kandler far right) and employees.

A typical small grocery store of the late 1930s—Kandler's Foods, at 7404-06 W. Irving Park Road. From left to right: William Kandler, (Unknown), Walter Schoenfeld (1st Fire Chief), John Bockholt, Lil Moen and Myrtle Radtke.

In 1937, the owner of the Acacia Park Cemetery sold half of the land, running from the center of Montrose Avenue, to one of his associates, and on this land was founded the Westlawn Jewish Cemetery. In 1938, when Depression conditions had begun to ease up, a development company, Duro-craft Homes, created a sub-division on land south of Foster Avenue and west of Harlem, taking in what are now Octavia, Oconto, and Odell streets. A few families began to move into the seventy-some houses built there. In

63

Westlawn Jewish Cemetery was founded in 1937.

that same year, Michael Enright built a tavern at the corner of Oriole and Foster, which is still standing as the Landmark Pub.

The Great Depression lasted officially from 1929 to 1939. By 1940 the nation's business was perking up and more and more jobs were available, largely because more and more military material was being produced, due to the seriousness of the world situation. In Europe, Nazi Germany had conquered Poland, France, Norway, Denmark, Belgium and Holland, and was battering Great Britain with air raids to weaken it for an invasion. In the East, the Japanese Empire had occupied much of China and was making certain demands of the United States. Most people felt it wouldn't be long before the U.S. was drawn into war, and the nation was preparing for it.

On a Sunday afternoon, December 7, 1941, it came. Many of the farmers and homeowners of the future Harwood Heights and Norridge area were probably relaxing as people generally did then on a Sunday afternoon, sitting in an easy chair and listening to the radio. Many were perhaps tuned in to the Chicago Bears versus Chicago Cardinals football game being played at old Comiskey Park that day. Suddenly, the announcer broke in to report that news had just arrived that the American naval base at Pearl Harbor, Hawaii, had been bombed in a sneak attack by hundreds of Japanese warplanes, with a dreadful loss of American lives, and serious damage to the U.S. fleet. Thus, World War Two began for America.

World War Two was treated with a great deal more seriousness than World War One had been, for there was real danger that the United States

Mike Enright, founder of the tavern built at 5135 N. Oriole Avenue in 1938, which today is the Landmark Pub.

The Landmark Pub. 1950.

Mike Enright and several residents of the area in 1940, displaying the Norwood Park Township Volunteer Fire Department vehicle.

could be invaded and that it could lose Hawaii and Alaska. While a little more than 2½ million men had been drafted into service during World War One, there were nearly ten million drafted during World War Two, and millions more enlisted. A number of men from the Norridge-Harwood Heights area served in the military forces during the war, including even the Reverend Addy of Acacia Park Lutheran Church, who entered the service in 1943 as a military chaplain. Richard Phillips, of the Phillips family that had come into the Norridge area in 1873, served in the Marine Corps, and Charles Kuhn, a Harwood Heights area resident since 1936, spent three years in the navy. And there were others. There were also losses. The Van Bergens, who had been in the area since 1890, lost one of their young men, who was killed in action in the Phillipine Islands, early in the war.

With millions of men and women in the armed forces, and millions of others working in "defense plants"—factories producing military supplies— farmers were often hard-pressed to get the help they needed. This was especially true for the truck farmers of the Harwood Heights-Norridge area. But the problem was solved, as it was in other parts of the nation as well, by permitting German prisoners-of-war, many thousands of whom had been brought to the United States after the surrender of German forces in Africa, to work on farms. They were glad to do so, both because it gave them something to do and because they were paid wages which enabled them to buy cigarettes and other luxuries. It was a common sight, in the later years of the war, to see scores of these men, in their uniform tan clothing, working

Robert L. Berner Co. (1942) was a Midwest nut mixing and distribution facility. The company also processed, packaged and shipped onion sets. Located at 4301 N. Harlem Ave.

in the fields that lay between Harlem and Cumberland, Irving Park and Foster. Some of these men, having seen the United States and liking what they saw, chose to return much later as immigrants, becoming American citizens.

Despite the abnormality of the war years, with their large-scale anxiety, grief, and turmoil, the small triumphs and tragedies of everyday continued in the Norridge-Harwood Heights area, as elsewhere. In 1942, the eyes of the nation's golf fans turned to the area, when the Hale American Tournament, an event equal to the National Open (which wasn't held that year) was held at Ridgemoor Country Club. The winner was famous golf-great Ben Hogan, who set a course record of 62. In the same year, a fire destroyed the building in which the congregation of the Acacia Community Presbyterian Church had been meeting. For a time, services were held in the Giles School, but under the leadership of the Rev. Roscoe Nahrle, property was soon purchased at the southwest corner of Oriole and Cullom, across from the school, and in 1944 ground was broken and work began on the church building which still stands at that site.

The war officially ended in September of 1945. Millions of young Americans began coming home, intent on building futures for themselves, getting married, having children, settling down in homes of their own. Because of this, within the next five years the population of the southwest corner of Norwood Park Township would literally grow like an explosion, and the two new villages of Norridge and Harwood Heights would come into existence.

The Acacia Community Presbyterian Church.

CHAPTER 5

THE BIRTH AND GROWTH OF THE TWO VILLAGES: 1946-1959

THE BIRTH AND GROWTH OF
THE TWO VILLAGES: 1946-1959

BY THE END of World War Two, most of the southwest corner of Norwood Park Township was still pretty much as it had been at the end of World War One. The region west of Harlem Avenue was mostly open farmland spotted with isolated farmhouses far apart from one another. The area east of Harlem was more farms, with a few milk stores at the edge of the road. A peony farm at Harlem and Gunnison, owned by a Judge Heckel, was a "landmark." The warehouse, "Onion Hall," which had been a factory during the war, stood by itself on the east side of Harlem Avenue. At the corners of Irving Park and Ozark and Irving Park and Olcott there were buildings that were gambling casinos. And huddled in one small area between Irving Park and Montrose, and another small area between Foster and Lawrence, were tiny residential sections of homes, close together.

Things began to stir a bit in the years just after the war. In 1947, a big outdoor motion picture screen went up on land at the corner of Harlem Avenue and Forest Preserve Drive, and the Harlem Avenue Outdoor Theatre opened for business. And here and there throughout the area, a number of other new business ventures began.

The farmers of the area were still satisfied with the way things were, but the people of the two tiny residential sections were not. The problems that had been plaguing homeowners in this unincorporated area for more than twenty years were, if anything, now worse. Unpaved streets were pitch-black from dawn to dusk and were rivers of mud in spring and summer and rutted stretches of snow and ice in winter. During heavy rains, many homeowners often had flooded basements. No police cars ever prowled through the area, and there was serious danger of fire because there weren't adequate facilities for water—it was almost impossible to even have a hot bath. Now that the war was over and things were getting back to normal, people wanted an end to these hardships; they wanted what citizens of established communities had—lighted, paved streets; police and fire protection; ade-

Harlem Irving Plaza and Harlem Outdoor Theater in the 1950s.

A "Field Day" at the James Giles School in about 1946.

Photo courtesy Giles School.

quate water; storm sewers. Once again, the idea of becoming annexed to Chicago was widely talked about. But now, people began trying to do something about it.

Herbert Huening, a World War Two veteran of three years active service in the navy, had moved into the area between Foster and Lawrence Avenues shortly after the end of the war. He joined with some of his neighbors to form an association to try to do something about the community's problems, and agreed to head a committee to find out how the community could get itself annexed to Chicago. Huening began visiting City Hall in Chicago, talking to politicians, showing petitions, asking questions. But it quickly became obvious to him that the people who ran Chicago really weren't very interested in annexing the little cluster of homes in the unincorporated area of Norwood Park Township. It would probably never happen.

However, there was another way of solving the problem, a way that Huening and some of his neighbors had talked about. This was for the community to become an incorporated area on its own, by officially becoming a village. The village could then raise money through taxes and in other ways, in order to have streets paved and lighted, sewers put in, and all the other needs taken care of. Huening went to work to find out what would have to be done to turn his community into a village.

By the fall of 1947 he had everything ready, and arranged to have the people of the area vote on whether or not they wished to incorporate as a village. The majority of votes—350—were in favor of incorporation. And so, the Village of Harwood Heights was conceived.

Herbert Huening, first Mayor of Harwood Heights and a guiding spirit behind the formation of the community.

Unfortunately, there is no official record of how, or by whom, the new village's name was chosen. Tradition has it that the "Har" portion comes from the first three letters of Harlem Avenue, while the "wood" is from Norwood. Another source indicates that the name was chosen because a number of homes in the area were built by a firm known as Harwood Builders. But the "Heights" part of the name is a total mystery.

Harwood Heights was officially chartered as a village, with a population of four hundred, on March 4, 1948. The village consisted of the four square blocks bounded on the north by Foster Avenue, on the south by Lawrence Avenue, on the east by Harlem Avenue, and on the west by Oketo Avenue. Herbert Huening was elected as the first village president.

In the same year Harwood Heights was founded, the Parish of St. Eugene Catholic Church, at Foster and Canfield, was also founded. The first pastor was Father John M. Ryan.

Meanwhile, the other residential area, between Irving Park Road and Montrose Avenue, was going through much the same sort of activities that Harwood Heights had gone through. There, a group of people had formed an organization they called the Annexation Improvement Club, which had been trying for several years to get the community annexed to Chicago, and had talked with 48 different Chicago aldermen during that time. At one point it looked as if their efforts would be successful, for the petition for annexation was tentatively accepted by the committee that took care of such things. But after a period of thirty days during which the little community was technically part of Chicago, the acceptance was withdrawn. In disgust

Norwood Park Township offices.

The home of Herbert Huening and the first Harwood Heights Village Hall.

The original St. Eugene Church.

The present day St. Eugene Church.

St. Eugene School.

at this, Joseph Sieb, a resident of the area since 1941, and one of the leaders in the move for annexation, suggested to the other members of the Club that they give up the idea of joining Chicago and solve their problems as Harwood Heights had done, by incorporating as a village. There was some disagreement at first, but eventually everyone recognized the merit of Sieb's suggestion. It was worked out that the village should consist of the area bounded on the north by Montrose Avenue, on the east by Harlem Avenue, on the South by Irving Park Road, and on the west by Ozanam Avenue. It would thus have the shape of a rectangle with a tiny bit of the southeastern corner sliced off on an angle by Forest Preserve Drive. For a village name, a Mrs. Link, one of the organization's members, suggested taking the "Nor" of Norwood Park, and the "Ridge" of nearby neighboring town Park Ridge, and joining them together to make the name Norridge.

**Karl A. Kuchar, first president
of the Village of Norridge.**

Joseph Sieb. He assumed the office of president of the Village of Norridge in 1951 and has served continuously for more than 35 years.
Photo courtesy Village of Norridge.

On December 4, 1948, a vote was taken within the community to see if a majority of the people wanted to form the proposed village. The result was 578 *for*, to 195 *against*. Thus, Norridge came into being. Its population was 3,028. The Annexation Improvement Club changed its name to Norridge Improvement Club, and put together a group of candidates to form the first government of the new village. Karl A. Kuchar became the first village president.

The governments and residents of the two new villages often had to "make do" and improvise as much as the early settlers of the nineteenth century had done. In Norridge, the first village "office" in which elected officials got together to work, was a room in the village clerk's home, and for the first five years, village meetings were held in the Norwood Park Township fire-

An aerial view of the Giles School in 1948. Construction of the first addition was underway.

house at 4348 Ottawa Avenue. Catholic residents of the communities attended Mass in the basement of the Giles School while they scrimped, saved, and worked to get a church built.

The first years of the nineteen fifties were a time of swift growth and improvement for both villages. Street lighting, paving, storm sewers, garbage pickup, water supply, and police protection were taken care of, not always easily. In 1951, Joseph Sieb became Norridge's village president, beginning a term of service that was to last more than thirty-five years, as he was re-elected time after time and was still serving into the second half of the nineteen eighties! Also in 1951, the area from Argyle Street to Ainslie Street, west of Harlem, was annexed by Harwood Heights, and in the following year the remaining portion of land south to Lawrence Avenue was also annexed. The first firm of Harwood Heights' Industrial Park, Magnaflux Corporation, was in place at 7300 West Lawrence in 1953. In 1954, Norridge annexed land north from Montrose to Lawrence, and development for housing began. Norridge also saw work begin on its first official village building, which contained two offices and a garage, and saw the completion of its new water system, which included a reservoir, a pumping station, and fire hydrants.

Growth and expansion caused school problems; as new families with small children settled in the new little towns, the area schools suddenly found themselves gaining forty or fifty new students in a single day, for whom there was not enough room. In 1950 an addition was built onto the Giles School, but that same year the Annex had to be closed for boiler repairs, and children who attended classes there had to be moved to Giles, filling it nearly to capacity. Union Ridge School was also at the bursting point, with 275 students in a building that held less than 200, ten years before.

To solve Union Ridge School's problem, the schoolboard provided for a sale of bonds to raise money for four new classrooms and a lunchroom to be added on. But by 1953 enrollment had jumped to 407, and more bonds

**Magnaflux Corporation, the first industrial complex
located in Harwood Heights in 1953.**

Aerial photo of Norridge and Harwood Heights in 1950. *Photo courtesy Chicago Aerial Survey.*

Carstens Health Industries, Inc., Breuer Electric Mfg. Co., and the Ansan Co. are located in Harwood Heights Industrial Park.

Among other firms located in the Harwood Heights Industrial Park are FCL Graphics, ADP and the Methode Company.

81

One of the first homes built in the area during the development boom in the 1950s. Built in 1950, this house stands near the corner of Lawrence and Ozanam Avenues, behind the Dunkin Donuts establishment.

had to be sold to raise money for a second floor to be built over the new additions! To solve the Giles School problem, "old time" Norridge resident John V. Leigh, who was now School District 80 Superintendent, managed to persuade building companies putting up new homes in the area to chip in and start constructing a new school, and also pushed to get the Annex renovated so that it could accomodate a lot more children. Unfortunately for this plan, a fire started in the Annex in the early morning hours of Sunday, June 21, 1953, and the building was completely destroyed. Leigh was thus forced to begin a "split shift" program at the Giles School until a new addition could be tacked onto the building, with some children attending school only half a day, in either the morning or the afternoon. The addition, at the school's north end, was finished in 1954 and the split shift was quickly abolished. Meanwhile, work on the new school, being built at 8151 West Lawrence Avenue, continued.

It was in 1954, by a special Village Resolution, that the Norridge Youth Activities Committee was formed to sponsor and assist in the promotion of athletic and social events—such as organized baseball, football, and basketball teams, dance classes, baton twirling groups, sewing classes, etc.— for boys and girls from the ages of eight to nineteen. In time, an annual "NYA Norridge Days Carnival" was held in the parking lot of the Harlem Irving Plaza, to raise money for NYA programs. All the work from the planning and administration of programs to the coaching of Little League teams, was done by volunteers from the area.

Stores and little shops were scattered throughout the area—a Jewel grocery store at the corner of Irving Park Road and Oriole, a drug store and National grocery store on the northeast corner of Lawrence and Cumber-

An aerial view of Giles School on Band Day in 1952 as seen looking north. Note the open farmland at top of picture where Divine Savior School and Church stand today. *Photo courtesy Giles School.*

The Giles School Annex was destroyed by fire on June 21, 1953.
Photo courtesy Norwood Park Fire District.

Canfield Avenue in 1951, as seen looking northwest from Lawrence Avenue.

land, and so on. But across the nation, the way people shopped was changing. "Shopping centers," with many stores and shops all bunched together, were being built in more and more communities. And in 1955, with the encouragement of Norridge President Sieb, developers began work on a shopping center at the corner of Harlem Avenue and Irving Park Road, which had been occupied by a miniature golf course and golf driving range. A search began for businesses that might be interested in coming into the area, and forty-five firms were quickly rounded up, a number of which were still to be found in the Harlem-Irving Plaza in the last portion of the 1980's— Famous Beauty Salon, Fannie May Candies, the Lerner Shop, William A. Lewis, Mailing Shoes, the Schiller Shop, Walgreen's, Wieboldt's, and Woolworth's. The shops were arranged in a single row forming an L shape with Wieboldt's at the corner. They were not enclosed at that time, and shoppers going from store to store had to contend with sizzling heat and pelting rain in summer and snow and sub-zero temperatures in winter.

A church and a school had their beginning in 1955. The church was the Church of the Open Door (now the Bethany Baptist Church of Harwood Heights) which was organized that summer, the Reverend Douglas Fisher the first pastor. For a time, services were held in the Edison Park American Legion Hall. The school was the fourth school to be named after early settler James Pennoyer; the present James Pennoyer School, construction of which was begun in 1955 in the still-unincorporated area at Cumberland and Foster Avenues.

1955 also saw the beginning of the Norridge Community Park District,

84

**Looking eastward along Lawrence Avenue from Ozaňam
Avenue in the foreground. 1954.**

with the purchase of twenty-two acres of land between Wilson and Lawrence
Avenues, and the completion of the first of the Divine Savior Parish buildings. The Divine Savior building was designed to be a school building to
house classrooms for the children of the parish, and the ground floor was
to be used only temporarily for Masses until a proper church could be built.
Father Walter Morris was the first pastor.

In 1956, the people of the unincorporated area east of Harwood Heights,
across Harlem Avenue, were suffering the common problems of an unincorporated area—no streetlights, no paving, no sewers, etc. An attempt to
incorporate as a village called Ridgemoor failed, as did an attempt to incorporate as the Village of Union Ridge. So, a majority of the people in the
area asked for annexation to a neighboring established village and were
joined to Harwood Heights that year. Shortly afterward, Chicago annexed
most of the remaining unincorporated land around the two villages, making
them an "island" surrounded by the city.

It was also in 1956 that the Central Baptist Home for the Aged moved
from Chicago onto nine acres of land in Norridge, at 7901 West Lawrence
Avenue, and that the Maurice Lenell Cookie Company built its factory at
4474 N. Harlem Avenue and began teasing Harwood Heights and Norridge
youngsters with lovely smells on windy days.

At this time, the newer portions of Norridge and Harwood Heights west
of Harlem Avenue still had much of the look of a country town. A number
of small, light industrial plants extended a short way from the corner of

The southeast corner of Lawrence and Ozanam Avenues in 1954.

Construction of the Harlem Irving Plaza began in the fall of 1955. A "Kiddieland," built in the late 1930s, stood on the adjoining land.

Photo courtesy Harlem Irving Realty.

**The present Bethany Baptist Church of Harwood Heights
under construction and finished.**

The present Pennoyer School, the fourth school to be named after early settler James Pennoyer, was completed in 1956. *Photo courtesy Pennoyer School.*

The Divine Savior Church building was completed in 1955.

Harlem and Lawrence Avenues, but most of the land from Harlem to Cumberland, between Montrose and Foster, was still farmland dotted with a few old farmhouses. The west side of Cumberland to Higgins road was a shaggy mass of forest, broken by a few small patches of farmland, while most of the east side from Montrose to Lawrence was lined with a number of stables at which horses could be hired for riding on the bridle path that ran through the forest preserve. At night, people driving west on Lawrence Avenue past Harlem had to rely entirely on their headlights to pick out the narrow, old-fashioned two-lane road; on all sides of them was total blackness broken only by the lights of a few farmhouses set back off the road.

New streets were going in from Lawrence to Montrose. Bulldozers and

The old Fire Department building located on Montrose and Ottawa.

The Fire Department personnel, with their equipment, outside the firehouse.
Photo courtesy Norwood Park Fire District.

cement mixers roared and rumbled, and a double row of houses began to go up. When the first five or so were completed, they were decorated, furnished, and opened for inspection, so that prospective buyers could select a house of the color and style they preferred, which would then be built further on down the street. "Settlers" were now pouring into the two villages in greater numbers than they ever had since the 1830's. Most of the men were World War Two veterans in their thirties, with families of two or three children of pre-school and early grade school age. They came from apartments in Chicago, where most of them were employed, and bought the new homes that went up along Oriole and the other new streets that were beginning to cut through the farmland.

**Central Baptist Home established 1956 and
the newest addition with a scenic pond.**

The famous Maurice Lenell cookie factory constructed in 1956.

The Norridge Village Hall, consisting of four offices, a council chamber, police headquarters and a garage, was dedicated in 1958.

Photo courtesy Village of Norridge.

Looking west on Gunnison Street between Pittsburgh and Pontiac Avenues on May 19, 1957, following a severe rainstorm.

In 1957, what is now the entire east end of Harwood Heights, to Nara-
gansett Avenue, was annexed. At 4301 Harlem Avenue, the big building
that had been a warehouse for farmers in the twenties, a dance hall and
gambling casino in the thirties, and a factory in the forties, now became
Stark's Warehouse, a store selling mainly surplus military equipment from
World War Two and the Korean War, which might be of use to civilians—
army and navy shoes, rainwear, blankets, tools, etc. During the year, the
upper floor of the new school at 8151 West Lawrence, which had been named
the John V. Leigh School in honor of the man who had been instrumental
in getting it built, was finished so that the first classes could be held in it
in September.

The lower floor of the school was completed in 1958, and in that same
year, the Union Ridge School District was annexed by Harwood Heights.
But while school problems were now pretty well solved for the younger
children of Norridge and Harwood Heights, there was still no high school,
of course, in either of the two communities. Thanks to a special permit for
which citizens of the two villages paid a special tax, young people of high
school age were able to attend classes in nearby high schools in Des Plaines
and Chicago. But in 1958 the Illinois General Assembly voted to abolish all
non-high school districts in the state, meaning that the communities of
Harwood Heights and Norridge would either have to form a school district
of their own, or would otherwise be assigned to an existing one, which could
be inconvenient for some of the students who might have to travel a long
way to get to the school to which they were assigned. However, a number
of people in the two villages had been working together with the idea of
creating a high school district and building a school, and they were quickly

Stark's Warehouse Store, a historic (but unattractive) area landmark, in 1980.

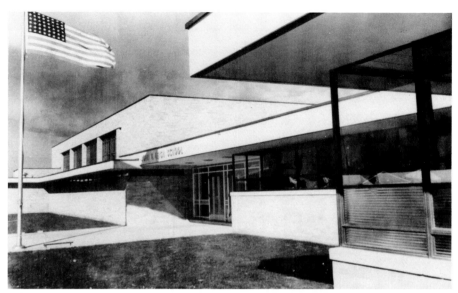

The John V. Leigh School was completed in 1959. *Photo courtesy Leigh School.*

able to offer a plan to the two communities. On July 12, 1958, by a majority of nearly three to one, the people of Harwood Heights and Norridge voted to establish a new high school district in the area, and to build a school that would actually be within walking distance for every young person living in the three square mile space of the two villages at that time. The site selected for the school was a section of open marshy land, scattered over with trees, which had been intended for development in the 1930's that never took place. A contest held to name the school resulted in the name "Ridgewood," a combination of the "ridge" of Nor*ridge*, and the "wood" of Har*wood*.

The building of the Church of the Open Door (now Bethany Baptist Church) was completed in 1958, at 6700 West Gunnison. It was also in 1958 that work began on the first St. Joseph's Ukrainian Catholic Church at 5000 North Cumberland Avenue. In 1956, Father Joseph Shary had been sent to organize a church for Ukrainian families on the northwest side of Chicago, and for a time Father Shary held Masses wherever he could, while his congregation slowly grew. Finally, in 1958, it was felt there were enough people, so work on a church building began and a special subdivision, known as St. Joseph's Manor, was developed nearby to provide homes for Ukrainian families that wished to live close to their church.

In August of 1958, a large newly built store, Goodman's Community Discount Department Store, opened up at 4731 North Harlem. Before long, it was known throughout the two communities as simply "Community."

93

In 1959, the new Pennoyer School in the unincorporated area asked for annexation to Norridge and became part of that village. It did not become part of the Norridge school system, however, remaining independent. In 1959, five tennis courts were constructed in the Norridge Community Park.

As things stood at the end of 1959, south of Montrose from Cullom to Olcott was the "old" established part of Norridge, with tree-lined streets and homes dating from the 1920's and 30's and east of Oriole, from Lawrence to Foster, was the established part of Harwood Heights, with more treelined streets and a collection of well-kept-up office and light industrial buildings. North of Montrose and west of Oriole sprouted the new town sections; rows of brand new houses standing on treeless lawns that were just beginning to show grass. In distant fields, farther north and west, bulldozers were still at work as new streets were being created and foundations of new homes dug. A number of churches of various denominations were scattered over the area; six grade schools, public and parochial, provided for the needs of the area's younger children; there was a small but thriving shopping center at the corner of Harlem Avenue and Irving Park Road, and a number of other useful stores and shops here and there on Harlem and Irving Park.

There were still many remnants of the past. The row of stables—the Greentree Stable, the Happy Days Riding Academy, and others—stretched along the east side of Cumberland Avenue, and here and there on shrunken farm fields among the rows of new houses, stood fifty and sixty-year old farmhouses, like aging chaperones surrounded by bustling, excited youngsters at a high school dance. Their day was ending; the communities of Harwood Heights and Norridge were moving into the future.

The Community Discount Department Store in 1979. It stood on what is now the Harwood Square shopping area.

94

Descendants of Alexander Robinson, the Boettcher family, were still living in the area in 1948. Their house, pictured here, stood on what is now the Forest Preserve area bisected by the Des Plaines River.

CHAPTER 6

MOVING INTO MODERN TIMES: 1960-1980'S

MOVING INTO MODERN TIMES:
1960-1980'S

THE EARLY 1960's were largely a time of openings and completions in the two communities. In 1960, the St. Rosalie Roman Catholic Church opened its doors for the first time, at 4401 North Oak Park Avenue in Harwood Heights, its first pastor, Father Clement H. Conrad; and in Norridge, the First Baptist Church of Norridge opened at 4701 North Canfield Road, with the Rev. Walter Schmidt its first pastor. That same year, in September, Ridgewood High School opened, with a student body that consisted entirely of Freshmen and Sophomores. The school's first superintendent was Eugene V. Howard, who had been Assistant Principal of the Laboratory Training School of the University of Illinois. A number of the paintings now hanging in Ridgewood and other area schools are the work of the first president of the Ridgewood school board, William R. McGowen, a businessman who was an enthusiastic amateur artist.

Within a few years after its opening, Ridgewood High was recognized by educators throughout the United States as actually one of the ten best high schools in the entire nation. The main reason for this was that Superintendent Howard established what was then a new system of teaching, based on the ideas of noted Illinois educator Dr. J. Lloyd Trump. Under this system, the school provided team-teaching, with which a student could get instruction in a particular subject from several instructors rather than just one, and could pursue his or her studies at the fastest pace possible instead of merely having to go along with the pace of the entire class. Thus, for example, students who found standard high school physics too easy, could study physics at college level on their own, with the help of several teachers. As Superintendent Howard put it, "We don't lock them in, we permit them to escape!" The Ridgewood system worked so well that educators from all parts of the nation and several foreign nations as well, came to study it, and the school was featured in a television documentary produced by WTTW (Channel 11, Chicago) on secondary education in the U.S. and Great Britain.

The St. Rosalie School and Convent under construction in 1964.
Photo courtesy St. Rosalie Church.

**Mr. Eugene V. Howard, first
Superintendent of Ridgewood
High School in 1960.**
Photo courtesy Ridgewood High School.

Ridgewood High School under construction in 1960.
Photo courtesy Ridgewood High School.

First Baptist Church of Norridge founded in 1964.

It was in 1960 that a serious financial problem led to the beginning of what was to become a yearly tradition in the two villages and the nearby area. Looking for a way to raise money that was badly needed for the St. Joseph Ukrainian Catholic Church on Cumberland Avenue, Father Joseph Shary decided to hold a carnival. Over the next twenty-five years and more, this became the annual "Fun fair," combining carnival games, rides, and atmosphere, with ethnic foods, entertainment, and folkways that represented some of the many nationalities to be found in the Harwood Heights-Norridge area.

It was also in 1960 that work was begun on the red brick buildings with their distinctive cupolas and weathervanes, which front Lawrence Avenue between Overhill and Ozanam Avenues in Norridge. They were completed in 1961. The largest building, at the corner of Lawrence and Ozanam, was originally an A&P (Atlantic and Pacific Tea Company) grocery store; one of a chain of food stores once widespread throughout the Chicagoland area, but now all long gone.

In 1961, the south addition to the Giles School was completed, housing Anderson Hall, the band room, and the nurse's room. In 1962, the Norridge Park District Pool was built, and in 1963, the first highrise building in the northwest suburbs, Parkway Towers, was completed. 1963 also saw the completion of the kindergarten wing, offices, and teachers' lunchroom sections of Giles School, and the opening of the St. Rosalie School in Harwood Heights. A new church also came into Norridge that year, with the building

The present Acacia Park Lutheran Church was constructed in 1960.

of the Zion Evangelical Lutheran Church at 8600 West Lawrence Avenue, the Rev. John Bajus its pastor. Although housed in a new building, it was not really a new church, for it was more than fifty years old in 1963, having stood at two locations in Chicago since the year 1909.

1964 saw the opening of the present Village Hall of Harwood Heights, and the completion of the vocational training and science rooms at Leigh School. In 1965, ground was broken for a $1,750,000.00 addition to Ridgewood High School, to house the science laboratories, industrial arts area, and a 31,000 square-foot library classroom.

In 1968 there was both an ending and two beginnings. The ending was that of the old Franzen farmhouse, which had stood on East River Road, between Foster and Bryn Mawr Avenues, for more than one hundred years, and which was now torn down. One of the beginnings was that of the Wesleyan Church of Norridge, which bought the Acacia Presbyterian Church building at 4526 North Oriole Avenue, renaming it, initially, the Christ Wesleyan Church. The first pastor was the Rev. Ronald W. Tery.

The other beginning was that of the Eisenhower Library, now serving the two communities of Harwood Heights and Norridge. There had been an attempt to form a library back in 1965, sparked by several of the area churches, but lack of general interest caused the project to be abandoned by those who had begun it. However, there were a number of citizens in the area who felt that a community without a library was a bit like a body without a brain, and who finally took up the task of providing one. In 1968

Anderson Hall, the south addition to the Giles School, completed in 1961.

A sledding hill (upper right) once stood in the Norridge Community Park, overlooking the playing fields. *Photo courtesy Norridge Park District.*

104

The Norridge Community Park swimming pool under construction in 1962.

Photo courtesy Norridge Park District.

Parkway Towers, shown under construction in 1963, was the first highrise building in the western suburbs of Chicago. *Photo courtesy Ted Szywala and Mitchell Kobelinski.*

The first completed structure of Parkway Towers.
Photo courtesy Ted Szywala and Mitchell Kobelinski.

106

Zion Evangelical Lutheran Church built in 1963. Church was founded in 1909.

The present Harwood
Heights Village Hall
opened its doors in 1964.

Finalists in the Eisenhower Library's "Name the Library" contest in 1969. Winner James Scallion is second from the right, Library Trustee Martin Schneider
is on the far left.

a group of people that included Ruth Igoe, Kay Kupczyk, Carole McKenzie, Joseph Patricelli, Toni Wolanin, Natalie Rothbart, Martin Schnieder, and others, formed an organization known as "Friends of the Library for Norridge-Harwood Heights," and began to do what was necessary to get a community library started. In 1969 they received permission to hold a drive for membership and funds, and in May of that year, to spark interest throughout the two communities, the Friends of the Library conducted a "Name the Library" contest in all the local schools. Sixth grader James Scallion of St. Rosalie School came up with the name judged the winner— Dwight D. Eisenhower Library; named, of course, after the man who had been 36th President of the United States, from 1953 to 1961, and supreme commander of Allied forces in Europe during World War Two. Ex-President Eisenhower had died in March of 1969, and the Friends of the Library sought permission from his widow, Mrs. Mamie Eisenhower, to name the library after him. Permission was, of course, granted.

Also in 1969, work began on the Norridge theatres. Building was completed in 1970.

After two years of hard work, the library, under the direction of its first Director, Fred Donnelly, received a federal grant of $129,000.00, provided through the state Suburban Library System, and was able to buy books and equipment, hire workers, rent an area, and open its doors to the book-seeking people of Harwood Heights and Norridge.

The library's first home was a tiny, dreadfully cramped space on the

The Norridge Theater, completed in 1970, orginally housed 4 screens. Today there are 10 screens.

Fred Donnelly, first library director of the Eisenhower Library, in his office at the library's Parkway Towers location in 1974.

Fred Donnelly, Linda Woyner, Steve Olderr, and Collette Block next to first bookmobile and outside Parkway Towers site of first library facility in 1972.

Some of the library's founders. Standing left to right: Martin Schneider, William Wisniewski and Joseph Patricelli; seated left to right: Natalie Rothbart, Ruth Igoe and Catherine Kupczyk.

ground floor at the rear of the Parkway Towers building. Both to help with the storage and circulation of books and to make residents of the area more aware of the library, a bookmobile—a buslike truck containing shelves for hundreds of books—was rented from the Suburban Library System. A librarian would drive the bookmobile to various parts of Norridge and Harwood Heights each day, and open it up for residents to pick out books and take them home, just as if they had gone to the library itself.

It was at about this time that United States involvement in the Vietnam War was at its height. More than half a million American servicepeople were in Vietnam from 1965 to 1973, and there were many young men from Harwood Heights and Norridge among them. Some families in both communities suffered losses. George Gavaria, son of Mr. and Mrs. Albina Gavaria of Harwood Heights, died of wounds received in combat and was posthumously awarded six decorations, including the Bronze Star for Valor.

A hero of the Vietnam War. George L. Gavaria of Harwood Heights died of wounds received in combat and was posthumously awarded six decorations, including the Bronze Star for Valor.
Photo courtesy Gavaria Family.

In 1973 the Eisenhower Library set up a vote to determine if the residents of Harwood Heights and Norridge would allow all library expenses to be paid with a portion of the taxes they paid to their villages, as is done for the public libraries of most towns and cities. The referendum passed, and by the following year the library was being fully supported by tax money. That year, it was able to buy its own bookmobile and also to move to much larger quarters—an empty building that had been a sheet-metal factory, at 4652 N. Olcott.

In that same year, work began on the new home of the St. Joseph Ukrainian Catholic Church on Cumberland Avenue. Paster Shary hoped it would be "the most beautiful Ukrainian church in the world," and the work

Construction on the St. Joseph Ukrainian Catholic Church, with its unique dome structure, was started in 1973.

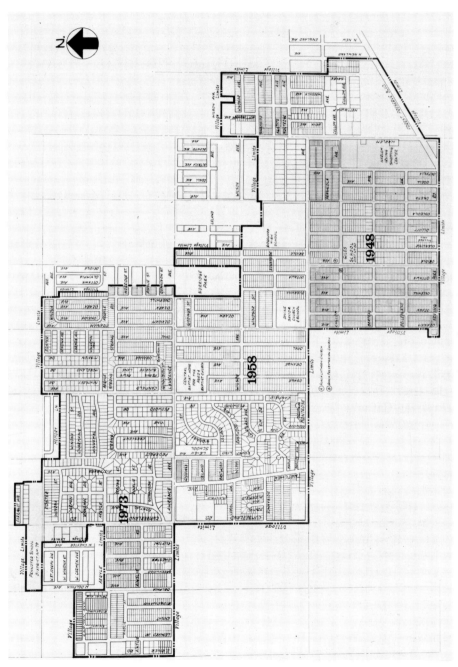

Village of Norridge, annexation and growth years 1948, 1958 and 1973.

The Norridge Community Park field-house, built in 1974, is dedicated to Carl H. Fredrickson Builders who do-nated time, labor and materials.
Photo courtesy Norridge Park District.

of 34 architects had been considered before the designs of a young Ukrainian-American man were finally accepted. His design, which now catches the eyes of most passing motorists, is a blend of both modern ideas and the medieval style of Ukrainian architecture and is intended to symbolize a free, united Ukraine.

Work for a giant expansion program for the Harlem-Irving Plaza began in 1975, and in 1976, sixteen new stores were opened. That same year, the Eisenhower Library, which had been renting the building on Olcott, was able to buy it, so the library finally had its permanent home. The bookmobile, no longer needed, was sold in December of 1975. The last bookmobile driver, Ron Stoch, later became the Library Director..

Meanwhile, at the other end of the two communities, problems were seething. Developers were seeking to buy up the land at Cumberland and Montrose on which the old Happy Day Stables stood, to turn the area into a new shopping center. However, homeowners living nearby were arguing against this, complaining that the village was becoming *overdeveloped*! But the stable's lease was up that fall and the owner refused to renew it. Horses and equipment were removed and the stables stood empty. On a night in September, someone deliberately set fire to them and most were burned down. Unwilling to have such unsightly and dangerous ruins near their dwellings, most of the homeowners ended their objections, and the Norridge village government urged the developers to tear down the charred remains and proceed with their plans. Thus, work commenced on the area that was

114

The Red Lobster was built in 1976.

The Eagle Food Center arrived in 1976.

to hold the Red Lobster Restaurant and the Eagle grocery store and adjoining stores.

The next few years saw a lot of tearing down and rebuilding in the two villages. In 1977, the thirty-year old Harlem Avenue Outdoor Theatre was torn down and work began on the Norridge Commons shopping area. Meanwhile, across the street at the Harlem-Irving Plaza, work was progressing on a new wing that would hold twenty-eight more stores, and on a ramp and rooftop parking area for cars. In 1978, the Eisenhower Library began a remodeling program of its new home, and in 1979 the twenty-year old Goodman's Community Discount Store was torn down so that work might begin on Harwood Heights' new Harwood Square shopping center.

In August of 1979, as the result of a merger, the Church of the Open Door, at 6700 W. Gunnison, became the Bethany Baptist Church of Harwood Heights. Also in 1979, a saddening event took place, when the sixty-four-year old Giles family farmhouse, at 7646 Lawrence Avenue, was destroyed by fire, apparently set by vandals. The land on which the farmhouse sat had been purchased as the site of the condominium which now occupies it, but the developers were quite willing to hold off from demolishing the house if it could be moved elsewhere, and some effort was underway to have it moved onto donated land where it could become an historical museum for the area. Unfortunately, there was not enough general interest in this project to get it moving very quickly, and it died aborning when the house was destroyed by the blaze. Thus, a genuine landmark and visible link with the past was lost forever. A tiny "Candy Cane Park," offering a slide and

Norridge Commons, established in 1977, includes Dominick's, Walgreens, Venture, Columbia National Bank and many small shops.

Harlem-Irving Plaza added a new wing in 1977.
Photo courtesy Harlem-Irving Realty Inc.

swings for very small children, which had stood for some time at the opposite corner of the block from the Giles house—the northwest corner of Lawrence and Oriole—was also lost when the condominum went up.

And still another historical landmark, of sorts, was also lost to fire in 1980, when Stark's Warehouse, the squarish one-story, ramshackle building at 4301 N. Harlem burned down. It was far from beautiful—in fact, it was rather ugly—but its roots were deep in area history. It had been a store, factory, dance hall, gambling casino, and storehouse for the produce of local farmers; and when its remains were torn down and removed, the appearance of the area may have improved, but some fifty years of local history and folklore were gone.

Harwood Square construction began in 1979 and includes K-Mart, Marshalls, as well as other shops.

Eisenhower Library remodeled and expanded the building which originally was a sheet metal factory.

In 1981 the Norridge Little League girls 12 inch softball team concluded a very successful season by winning the Illinois State Championship.

In 1985, the Axle Roller Rinks closed its doors forever. This brought a touch of nostalgic sadness to not only Norridge and Harwood Heights "old timers," but also to many other people throughout the entire Chicagoland area. For the Axle had begun its existence as the Hub Roller Rinks in the days of the Korean War (1950-1953), and many people could remember good times there during those years, when an evening at the roller rink had been a great source of fun for young soldiers, sailors, and marines, and their girlfriends.

1986 was a banner year for sports in Norridge and Harwood Heights,

Built in 1915, this house stood at what is now about 7700 Lawrence Avenue. At one time it was owned by the Giles family. Destroyed by fire in 1979.

Condominium complex at Lawrence and Overhill built on Giles farmhouse site.

thanks to the overwhelming success of a Little League baseball team made up of eleven and twelve-year old boys from the two communities. The team, representing the Norridge Youth Activities Little League program, won the Illinois State Championship, went on to win the Midwest Regional Championship—competing with the championship teams of nine other midwest states—and achieved fifth place in the Little League World Series playoffs held in Williamsport, Pennsylvania. The team was managed by Medard Zabratanski, Assistant Police Chief of Norridge, with the help of coach Kevin Ryan of Harwood Heights.

1987 became known to people of the Des Plaines River area as "the year of the big flood." Torrential autumn rains caused the river to rise and

Oriole Point condominium, built on the site of "Candy Cane Park" and near the Giles home, was completed in 1980.

The Norridge Community Park playground area under construction in 1980.

The Joe Sieb Community Center was dedicated in 1984.

overflow its banks, putting streets of some river-area communities under water and forcing many people out of their homes. While neither Norridge nor Harwood Heights suffered such catastrophe, water-filled streets were only a few blocks away from some of the westernmost parts of Norridge, causing concern, and many residents of both villages found themselves with flooded basements.

Several landmarks of the area, some quite old and some fairly recent, were lost in the late 1980's. For nearly thirty years a gasoline filling station had occupied the southwest corner of Oriole Avenue and Montrose Avenue; in 1986 this was replaced by a small building housing a number of offices. One block farther west, at Ottawa and Montrose, the building that had housed the Norwood Park Fire District Station 1 for several decades became empty in the summer of 1988 when all equipment and furnishings were moved from there and from Fire Station 2, at 7301 W. Lawrence Avenue, to a brand new building at 7447 W. Lawrence, in Harwood Heights. The new building stands on ground that was previously occupied, for about 35 years, by a factory. The old Fire Stations 1 and 2 were designated to become police stations for the police of Norridge and Harwood Heights respectively.

Holiday Bowl, a spacious 72-lane bowling alley that had stood at 4747 N. Harlem Avenue since 1959, was torn down in the summer of 1988 to make way for the twenty-store shopping center that was fittingly named Holiday Plaza. A short distance south on Harlem Avenue, at 4600, a large building that had, for several decades, housed first a Republic Lumber Company outlet and then a Joseph Lumber Company outlet, was also partially torn down in the summer of 1988 in order to convert the site into another shopping mall.

And still another shopping area, Dunning Square, was also begun in 1988, on land that had been part of the Dunning Hospital grounds, at Irving Park Road and Narragansett Avenue. The land, comprising a total of twenty-eight acres, had been purchased from the state by the Village of Norridge, which then sold thirteen acres to the Harlem-Irving Realty Company, owner of the Harlem-Irving Plaza, and fifteen acres to Ray Venture Limited, for

A flooded Lawrence Avenue, west of East River Road, was closed to traffic for several days. Very few bridges crossing the Des Plaines River were passable during the flood of '87, thus forcing drivers to travel extra miles and creating many traffic jams.

the construction of a housing development adjoining the plaza. Old red-brick buildings that had stood on this site for some three-quarters of a century, and which had housed tens of thousands of patients over the decades, were torn down. Meanwhile, an adjoining section of the former Dunning grounds, at Montrose and Narragansett Avenues, became the site for the new campus of Wright Junior College.

Extensive changes were made in the Harlem-Irving Plaza in 1987 and 1988. In 1987 a fifteen-month project to renovate the north wing was completed, with a number of new stores added, including the Main Street Department Store building, and a new upper-level parking deck area. When the Harlem Irving Plaza had first opened in 1956, its main store had been a Wieboldt's department store, one of the newest stores of a highly successful chain that had been doing business in the Chicago area since the early days of the century. But in the latter part of the 1980's the Wieboldt chain suffered serious reverses and finally declared bankruptcy, closing the Harlem-Irving store and other stores in 1987. In 1988 the vacant store was taken over and remodeled as a new outlet of another department store chain long known in the Chicago area, Carson Pirie Scott and Company.

By the end of the 1980's, little was left of the country farm community that made up the area for more than a hundred years from the 1830's to 1950's. From the nineteenth century there is the red-brick Phillips house, just inside the cemetery fence at 4214 Ozanam; the remodeled farm house at 7710 W. Irving Park Road which is reported to be as much as 125 years old; the strip of woods along the Des Plaines River that was Che Che Pin Qua's reservation; and a few faint remnants of Israel Smith's farm on the land of the Ridgemoor Country Club. The country club itself is about the

The office complex built in 1986 at Ottawa and Montrose Avenues.

only reminder from the early 1900's, and from the 1920's there is only the original James Giles School building, the cemeteries, and some of the homes north of Irving Park, between Ozanam and Oriole. From the thirties there is the Landmark Pub, part of the Union Ridge School, and a few of the homes south of Foster Avenue, between Harlem and Oriole. All else really belongs to the "new time" of the area, the time of the two villages, from 1950 on.

Most of the problems that vexed people of the area in the days when Harwood Heights and Norridge first came into existence have long been solved, of course. But at least one remains—the problem of noise caused

The new Norwood Park Fire District station located on Lawrence Avenue, completed in 1988. The tall structure in the rear of the building is the firehouse cleaning room.

by airplanes taking off and landing at O'Hare Airport. Newspaper articles preserved from the early 1950's describe Norridge and Harwood Heights residents as halting their conversations and wincing as incoming or outgoing planes roared overhead, and the passage of some thirty years has not changed things much. In 1984, Norridge and Harwood Heights joined with eleven other suburban communities surrounding the airport, in bringing suit to halt plans for expansion of the airport, which would almost certainly increase the noise problem, but in 1986 the U.S. Court of Appeals rejected their pleas. It seems likely that this noise problem, which in some parts of the two villages is the equivalent of the sound of a vacuum cleaner at a

The spacious 72-lane Holiday Bowl, since 1959, was replaced in 1988 by Holiday Plaza.

distance of only ten feet, will be one of the few historical features of the area to carry into the twenty-first century!

Harwood Heights and Norridge today are fairly typical midwest-American suburbs; well-established, prosperous, and no longer really looking toward the future, but fitting comfortably into the present. However, history is an ongoing process—today's happenings are tomorrow's history. In a relatively short time, both villages will be marking their fifty-year anniversaries, and there is no way of telling what parts of the present villages may be revered historical landmarks fifty years from then, or seventy, or one-hundred. And, just as we wonder about the Indians who once built campfires where our village streets now crisscross, and about the early settlers who lived in this area when it was part of a vast prairie, people of future generations may wonder about us, who, long before they were born, lived in these two communities that form an island within a city.

Holiday Plaza parking lot with Parkway's two towers in background.

Harlem Plaza replaces Joseph Lumber Company which was once Republic Lumber Company.

The new Dunning Square and housing development being built on the Dunning Hospital grounds.

Construction activity at the Main Street department store was completed in 1987.

A branch of Wright Junior College will be built at Montrose and Narragansett Avenues on which was once Dunning Hospital property.

The new upper deck parking area at the Harlem-Irving Plaza was added to accommodate the additional shoppers.

127

The area's oldest home, the Phillips farmhouse, built before the turn of this century, stands on the Acacia Park Cemetery grounds at 4214 N. Ozanam Avenue.

The remodeled farmhouse at 7710 W. Irving Park Road is reported to be as much as 125 years old.

Harlem Irving Plaza (HIP) new sign featuring Carson Pirie Scott.

Union Ridge School built in the 1930s is a landmark from that era.

Montrose Avenue looking west. The Norridge water tower in background has a kiddie park adjacent to it.

Norridge Village Hall in 1988.

Thompson's bakery and grocery store, a landmark since 1944.

Rolling Stones record store.

Cumberland Chapels built in 1986.

Mini shopping area located on Montrose and Oriole Avenues.

Norridge Park District's park bench
and flagpole relaxation area.

Harwood Square shopping center located on Harlem Avenue
just north of Gunnison on the site of Roman Inc., 1987.

The new McDonald's on Harlem Avenue.

132

THE PARADE CELEBRATING HARWOOD HEIGHTS' 40TH ANNIVERSARY—1987

All photographs courtesy Judi Norrick

Grand Marshall Edna Vlchek, long-time resident of Harwood Heights.

The Rosie Posies Kitchen Band.

The Scottish Bagpipe Band.

Ridgewood High School Band.

Indian costume paraders.

1987 Junior League Illinois champions represented by team members from both Harwood Heights and Norridge.

135

Karen's School of Acrobatics and Dance.

Ray Willas.
Photo courtesy Village of Harwood Heights.

BIBLIOGRAPHY

Andreas, Alfred Theodore. *History of Cook County, Illinois: from the earliest period to the present time.* A. T. Andreas, 1884.

Bretz, J. Harlen. *Geology of the Chicago Region.* State Geological Survey Bulletin No. 65, Part 1. State of Illinois, 1939.

Hayner, Don and McNamee, Tom. *Streetwise Chicago: a history of Chicago street names.* Loyola University Press, 1988.

Heise, Kenan and Edgerton, Michael. *Chicago, Center for Enterprise.* 2 vols. Windsor Publications, 1982.

Kirkland, Joseph. *The Story of Chicago.* Dibble Publishing Co. 1892.

Edited by Moses, John and Kirkland, Joseph. *The History of Chicago, Illinois.* Munsell & Co., 1895.

Quaife, Milo M. *Chicago's Highways Old and New: from Indian Trail to Motor Road.* D. F. Keller, 1923.

INDEX

A

A & P, 102
ADP, **81**
Abolitionist movement, 33
Acacia Community Presbyterian
  Church
  See Churches
Acacia Park Cemetery
  See Cemeteries
Acacia Park Lutheran Church
  See Churches
Addy, A. Roy, Rev., 59, 66
Ague, 23, 24
Ainslie Street, 78
Anderson Hall
  See Schools
Annexation Improvement Club, 74,
  76, 77
Ansan Co., **80**
Argyle Street, 78
Armour, Tommy, 56
Aux Plaines River
  See Des Plaines River
Axle Roller Rinks, 118

B

Bajus, John, Rev., 103
Ball, Arza, 34
Ball, Charles, 22, 41
Ball, Drusilla, 34
Ball, Jessie, 33, 34, 41
Ball, Zebina, 34
Baseball, 82, 118, 119, **135**
Beecher, Henry Ward, 36
Bergen, Gerhard van, 43, 46
Bergen, John van, 43, 66
Bergen, Peter van, 43, 66
Berner Co. (Robert L.), **66**, 71
Bethany Baptist Church of Harwood
  Heights
  See Churches
Blackhawk, Chief, **21**
Blackhawk War of 1832, 21, **21**
Block, Collette, **110**
Bockholt, John, 63
Boettcher family, **95**
Bookmobile, **110**, 111, 112, 114
Breuer Electric Mfg. Co., 80
Brooks, Gardner, 20
Brooks Road, 27

Brooks Tavern, 27
Bryn Mawr Avenue, 103
Burhans, Solomon, 34
Burnett, William, 10

C

Candy Cane Park, 116, 117, **119**
Canfield Avenue, 26, 29, 37, 49, 51,
  57, 74, **83**, 99
Capone, Al, 62
Carson Pirie Scott and Co., 122, **129**
Carstens Health Industries, Inc., **80**
Cemeteries
  Acacia Park Cemetery, 42, **43**,
    55, 63, 123, **128**
  Union Ridge Cemetery, 20, 25
  Westlawn Jewish Cemetery, 63,
    64, 123
Central Baptist Home for the Aged,
  37, 85, **90**
Che Che Pin Qua
  See Robinson, Alexander
Checagou River
  See Chicago River
Chevalier, Catherine, 21, **39**
Chicago, 12-14, 19, 20, 22, 23, 33, 34,
  37, 38, 42, 57, 89, 92, 93
  Annexation, 59, 60, 73, 74, 76, 85
  Village, 12, 13
  Fire, 37, 38
  Massacre, 7-11
Chicago Bears, 64
Chicago Cardinals, 64
Chicago Northwestern Railroad, 36
Chicago River, 3, 4, 6, 12
Chicago State Hospital, 53
Chippewa Indians, 13
Christ Wesleyan Church
  See Churches
Church of the Open Door
  See Churches
Churches
  Acacia Community Presbyterian
    Church, 58, 59, 67, **67**, 103
  Acacia Park Lutheran Church,
    59, **61**, **103**
  Bethany Baptist Church of
    Harwood Heights, 84, **87**,
    93, 115
  Christ Wesleyan Church, 103

INDEX

Church of the Open Door, 84, 93, 115

Divine Savior Church, 85, 88

Episcopal Church of Norwood Park, 59, **61**

First Baptist Church of Norridge, 99, **102**

St. Eugene Church, 74, **75**

St. Joseph Ukrainian Catholic Church, 93, 102, 112, **112,** 114

St. Paul Evangelical Lutheran Church, 51, 52

St. Rosalie Church, 20, 99

Wesleyan Church of Norridge, 103

Zion Evangelical Lutheran Church, 102, 103, **107**

Civil War, 25, 33-35

Cleaver, George, Rev., 59

Columbia National Bank, **116**

Community Discount Department Store, 93, **94,** 115

Condominiums, **118, 119**

Conrad, Clement H., Rev., 99

Cook County, 13, 26-28, 60

Cook, Daniel Pope, 12, **12,** 13

County Farm, 28, 29, 36, 37, **45**

Crops, 12, 22, 23, 41, 52, 57, 58, 60

Cullom Avenue, 58, 59, 67, 94

Cumberland Avenue, 22, 27, 67, 82, 84, 88, 94, 102, 114

Cumberland Chapels, **131**

D

Dance hall, 92, 117

Dances, 62, 92, 94

Depression of 1893, 44

Depression of 1929, 60, 62-64

Des Plaines River, 3, 19, 21, 27, 119, 120, **121,** 122

Des Plaines, Village of, 92

Detroit, 7, 11

Divine Savior Church
See Churches

Divine Savior School
See Schools

Dominick's Finer Foods, **116**

Donnelly, Fred, 109, **110**

Dunkin Donuts, 82

Dunlap, George, 26, 35-37, 40

Dunlap, Mary, 26

Dunlap, William, 26

Dunning, Andrew, 37

Dunning Hospital, 36, 37, **45,** 52, 53, 54, 55, 121, 122, **126, 127**

Dunning Square, 121, **126**

Durocraft Homes, 63

DuSable, Jean Baptiste Point, 6, **7**

E

Eagle Food Center, 115, **115**

East River Road, 19, 22, 27, 103

Edison Park American Legion Hall, 84

Egghead Discount Software, **40**

Eisenhower, Mamie, 109

Eisenhower Public Library District, 103, **108,** 109, **110,** 112, 114, 115, **117**

Enright, Michael, 64, **65**

Episcopal Church of Norwood Park
See Churches

F

FCL Graphics, **81**

Famous Beauty Salon, 84

Farms, 22, 23, 26, 29, **45**
  Ball, 22
  Bergen, 43, **52**
  Brooks, 20
  Drewes, 50
  Dunlap, 26
  Franzen, 19, **52,** 103
  Giles, 37, 54, 115-117, **118**
  Grant, 29
  Guthier, 41, 42
  Harris, 43
  Hemingway, 34
  Horton, **56**
  Kline, 26
  Miller, 29
  Noble, 19
  Pennoyer, 22
  Phillips, 42, 43, 55, **57,** 122, **128**
  Rowley, 22
  Sass, 41
  Sherman, 19
  Smith, 19, 20, 52, 122
  Tanner, 22

INDEX

Farmhouses, 23, 29, 42, 50, 51, 66, 67, 71, 88, 89, 94
  Bergen, **52**
  Boettcher, **95**
  Franzen, **52**
  Giles, **118**
  Horton, **40**
  Lueth, **128**
  Phillips, **128**
  Sells, **51**
Fire Department
  See Norwood Park Fire Department
First Baptist Church of Norridge
  See Churches
Fisher, Douglas, Rev., 84
Flood, 119, 120, **121**
Foot, Elizabeth, 26
Foot, John, 26
Foot, John, Jr., 26, 34, 41, 49
Forest Preserve, 38-40, 88, **95**
  Che Che Pin Qua Woods, 21
  Catherine Chevalier Woods, 21
  Robinson Woods, 21
Forest Preserve Drive, 28, 71, 76
Fort Dearborn, 6-8, **8**, 9-13, 20
Fort Wayne, 7
Foster Avenue, 21, 22, 63, 64, 67, 71-74, 84, 88, 94, 103, 123
Franzen, Emma, 19
Franzen, Fredrick, 19
Franzen, Gerhardt, 19, 49
Franzen, Herman, 19
Franzen, John Henry, 19
Fredrickson, Carl H., **114**
Friends of the Library for Norridge-Harwood Heights, **108**, 109
Fun Fair, 102

G

Gambling casinos, 62, 66, 71, 92, 117
Gavaria, Albina, 111
Gavaria, George, 111, **112**
Giles, James, **36**, 37, 54, 56-58
Giles School
  See Schools
Giles School Annex
  See Schools
Golf driving range, 84
Goodman's Community Discount Department Store, 93, 115

Grant, C. P., 29
Grant, Martha, 29
Greentree Stable, 94
Griffith, William, 10, 11
Grocery stores, **63**, 82, 84, 102, 104, 115, **115**, **116**, **130**
Gunnison Street, 27, 41, 71, **91**, 93, 115
Guthier, Lawrence, 41

H

Hagan, Walter, 56
Hale American Tournament, 67
Happy Days Riding Academy, 94, 114
Harlem Avenue, 22, 27-29, 34, **50**, 54, 55, 57, 60, 62, 63, 67, 71, 73, 74, 76, 78, 84, 85, 88, 93, 94, 117, 120, 123, **132**
Harlem Avenue Outdoor Theatre, 71, **72**, 115
Harlem Irving Plaza, **72**, 82, 84, **86**, 94, 114, 115, **116**, 121, 122, **127**, **129**
Harlem-Irving Realty Company, 121
Harlem Plaza, 120, 121, **125**
Harris, Frederick, 43
Harris, Ralph, 55
Harwood Builders, 74
Harwood Heights' anniversary parade, **133-136**
Harwood Heights Industrial Park, 78, **80**, **81**, 94
Harwood Heights, Village of, 73, 74, **75**, 76-78, **79**, 82, 84, 85, 88, 89, 92-94, 99, 102, 103, **108**, 111, 112, 115, 120, 123-125
Harwood Square Shopping Mall, **94**, 115, **117**, **132**
Hayride, 62
Heald, Nathan, 7-11, 20
Heald, Rebecca Wells, **9**, 10, 11, 20
Heckel, Judge, 71
Hemingway, Allen, 34
Hemingway, Harriet, 34
Higgins Road, 19, 26, 34, 57, 88
Hogan, Ben, 67
Holiday Bowl, 120, **124**
Holiday Plaza, 120, **124**, **125**
Howard, Eugene V., 99, **101**
Hub Roller Rinks
  See Axle Roller Rinks
Huening, Herbert, 73, **73**, 74, **75**

INDEX

I

Igoe, Ruth, 109, **111**
Illinois, 12-14, 19, 20, 26, 27, 33, 49, 92
Illinois Indians, 13
Immigrants
  German, 12, 16, 25, 50, 64
  English, 38, 45
  Jamaican, 55
  Ukrainian, 93
Irving Golf Club, 52, **53**
Irving Park Road, 21, 22, 27, 28, 36, 37, 42, 49, 50, 55, 59, 60, 62, 63, 67, 71, 74, 76, 82, 85, 94, 121-123

J

James Giles School
  See Schools
James Monroe Pennoyer School
  See Schools
Jefferson Park, 42, 52, 56
Jefferson Township, 19, 27, 28, 35, 40, 41, **45**
Jewel Food Stores, 82
Joe Sieb Community Center, **120**
John Kinzie Estates, 55
John V. Leigh School
  See Schools
Joseph Lumber Co., 121, **125**

K

K-Mart, **117**
Kandler's Dairy, **63**
Kandler's Foods, **63**
Kandler, William, **63**
Karen's School of Acrobatics and Dance, **136**
Kiddie Park, **130**
Kiddieland, **86**
Kinzie Estates
  See John Kinzie Estates
Kinzie, John, 6-8, 10, 11, **11**, 12, 20
Kline, Barbara, 26
Kline, Frederick, 41, 49
Kline, George, 49
Kline, Jacob, 26
Kuchar, Karl A., **76**, 77
Kuhn, Charles, 66
Kupczyk, Kay, 109, **111**

L

Lake Michigan, 3, 4, 6, 10-12, 19
LaLime, Jean, 6
Landmark Pub, 64, **65**, 123
Lange, August H., Rev., 51
Lawrence Avenue, 19, 22, 29, 37, 43, 50, **50**, 57, 71, 73, 74, 78, 82, **84**, 85, **85**, **86**, 88, 92, 94, 102-104, 115, 117, 120, **121**
Leigh, John V., 62, 82, 92
Leigh School
  See Schools
Lenell Cookie Co.
  See Maurice Lenell Cookie Co.
Lerner Shop, 84
Lewis Women's Apparel
  See William A. Lewis Women's Apparel
Leyden Township, 27, 28, 35, 40, 42, **45**
Leyden Township School Number 4
  See Schools
Library
  See Eisenhower Public Library District
Lightfoot, Street, 55
Lincoln, Abraham, 33, 35
Link, Mrs., 76
Little League, 82, 118, 119, **135**
Log cabins, 23, 24, **24**, 29

M

Mackinac Island, 7, 11
Magnaflux Corporation, 78, **78**
Mailing Shoes, 84
Main Street Department Store, 122, **126**
Ma-Ka-Tai-Me-She-Kia-Kiah
  See Blackhawk, Chief
Maps, 15, 45, 79, 113
Marshalls, **117**
Maurice Lenell Cookie Co., 85, **91**
McDonald's, **132**
McGowen, William R., 99
McKenzie, Carole, 109
Methode, **81**
Miami Indians, 7, 9
Milk stores, 62, **63**, 71, **130**
Miller, Melchior, 29
Miniature golf course, 84

INDEX

Mishigonong
  See Lake Michigan
Moen, Lil, **63**
Montrose Avenue, 54, 55, 57, 63, 71,
  74, 76, 78, 88, 94, 114, 120, 122,
  130, 131
Morris, Walter, Rev., 85

N

NYA Norridge Days Carnival, 82
Nahrle, Roscoe, Rev., 67
Narragansett Avenue, 55, 92, 121,
  122
National grocery store, 82
Noise pollution, 123-125
Norridge Commons, 115, **116**
Norridge Community Park District,
  84, 85, 94, 102, **104, 105,** 114, **114,**
  119, 130, 132
Norridge Improvement Club, 77
Norridge Theatre Corp., **40,** 109, **109**
Norridge, Village of, 74, 76-78, **79,**
  82, 84, 85, 88, 89, **91,** 92-94, 99,
  102, 103, 111, 112, **113,** 114, 115,
  117, 118, 120, 121, 123-125, **130**
Norridge Youth Activities
  Committee, 82
Norwood Park, 35, 36, 42, 52, 76
Norwood Park Township, 37, 40-42,
  49, 55, 58, 60, 67, 71, 73, 74, **74**
Norwood Park Township Fire
  Department, **63, 65,** 77, 78, **89,** 120,
  123

O

Oak Forest Hospital, 52
Oak Park Avenue, 41, 99
Oconto Avenue, 63
Octavia Avenue, 63
Odell Avenue, 63
O'Hare Airport, 49, 123-125
Oketo Avenue, 62, 74
Olcott Avenue, 7, 71, 94, **112,** 114
Old Leyden Indian Agency House, **28**
Old Plank Road, 27, 28, 36
Olderr, Steve, **110**
Onion Hall, 71
Oriole Avenue, 50, 58, 59, 64, 67, 82,
  89, 94, 103, 117, 120, 123, 124, **131**
Oriole Point Condominium, **119**

Ottawa Avenue, 78, 120
Ottawa Indians, 10, 13
Ouilmette, Antoine, 11, **11,** 12, 20
Overhill Avenue, 57, 59, 102
Ozanam Avenue, 28, 42, 43, 49, 50,
  55, 59, 76, **85, 86,** 102, 122, 123
Ozark Avenue, 71

P

Parade
  *See Harwood Heights' anniversary
  parade*
Park Ridge, 76
Parkway Towers, 102, **106, 110,** 111,
  125
Patricelli, Joseph, 109, **111**
Pennoyer, James Monroe, 22, **22, 23,**
  24, 26
Pennoyer, John, 22, 24
Pennoyer School
  See Schools
Pennoyer, Stephen, 22, 41
Pennoyer, Susan, 22, 24, 26
Phillips, Mary Ann, 42
Phillips, Richard, 66
Phillips Street, 42, 43, 49, 50
Phillips, Walter D., 41
Phillips, William, 42
Pittsburgh Avenue, **91**
Plank Road
  See Old Plank Road
Plank Road Company, 27
Police Departments, 120
Pontiac Avenue, **91**
Poor Farm
  See County Farm
Porter, George B., 13
Potawatomi Indians, 3, 4, **5,** 6-14, **14**
  Burial, **6**
  Food, 3, 4, **5**
  Housing, 4, **5**
  Trade, 6, 7, 13
  Treaty, 13, 20, 21
Prairie, 3, 4, **4,** 19, 26, 29
Prisoners-of-war, 66, 67

R

Radtke, Myrtle, **63**
Randolph Street Market, 57
Ray Venture Limited, 121

INDEX

Red Cross, 55
Red Lobster, 115, **115**
Republic Lumber Company, 121, **125**
Ridgemoor Country Club, 20, 53, **53**,
   54, 55, **55**, 56, 67, 122, 123
Ridgemoor, Village of, 85
Ridgewood High School, 93, 99, **101**,
   103
Ridgewood High School Band, **134**
Roadhouses, 62
Roads, 27, 28, 50, 55, 71, 88
Robinson, Alexander, 9, 10, **10**, 11,
   12, 20, 21, 35, 37-39, **39**, 40, 95
Robinson, Cynthia, 12
Robinson Reservation, 21, 22, 24, 38,
   45, 122
Rockford, 26
Roller rinks
   See Axle Roller Rinks
Rolling Stones record store, **131**
Roman, Inc., **132**
Rosie Posies Kitchen Band, **133**
Rothbart, Natalie, 109, **111**
Rowley, Aldric, 22
Rowley, Herman, 22, 28
Rowley, Herman, Jr., 22
Rowley, Sarah, 22
Rowley, William, 22
Ryan, John M., Rev., 74
Ryan, Kevin, 119

S

St. Eugene Church
   See Churches
St. Eugene School
   See Schools
St. Joseph's Manor, 93
St. Joseph Ukrainian Catholic Church
   See Churches
St. Paul Evangelical Lutheran
   Church
   See Churches
St. Paul Evangelical Lutheran School
   See Schools
St. Rosalie Church
   See Churches
St. Rosalie School
   See Schools
Sarazan, Gene, 56
Sass, John, 41, 58

Scallion, James, **108**, 109
Schiller Shop, 84
Schmidt, Walter, Rev., 99
Schneider, Martin, **108**, 109, **111**
Schoenfeld, Walter, 63
Schools
   Anderson Hall, 102, **104**
   Divine Savior, 85, 88
   Giles School Annex, 41, 42, 58,
      59, **59**, 78, 82, 83
   James Giles, 58, 59, 62, 67, **72**,
      77, 78, 82, 83, 102, **104**, 123
   James Monroe Pennoyer, 22, 26,
      43, 57, **58**, 84, 88, 94
   John V. Leigh, 92, **93**
   Leyden Township School Number
      4, 28
   Ridgewood, 93, 94, **101**, 103
   St. Eugene, 76
   St. Paul Evangelical Lutheran
      School, 53
   St. Rosalie, 20, 99
   Union Ridge, 41, **42**, 53, 57, 58,
      78, 92, 123, **129**
   Wright Junior College, 122, **127**
Scottish Bagpipe Band, **134**
Settlers, 14, 19-29, 49
   Blacksmiths, 26
   Boundaries, 26
   Diseases, 23, 24
   Food, 22, 23
   Housing, 23
Shary, Joseph, Rev., 93, 102, 112
Sherman, Nicholas, 19, 23
Sherman, Phineas, 19, 23
Sherman, Phineas, Jr., 19, 23
Sherman, William, 19, 23
Sieb Community Center
   See Joe Sieb Community Center
Sieb, Joseph, 76, **77**, 78, 84
Skunk Road, 27
Smith, Gustavus, 19
Smith, Henry, 20
Smith, Israel, 19, 20, **20**, 24, 26, 27,
   33, 37, 41, 49, 52, 122
Smith, Kittie, 41
Smith, Marcellus, 19, 27
Smith, Waldo, 20
Smiths Ridge, 20, **25**, 26
Smiths Road, 27, 41
Smiths schoolhouse, 41

INDEX

Social activities, 60, 62, 82, 92, 94, 102, 117, 118
Softball, 118
Sound Warehouse, **40**
South Water Street Market, 57
Stables, 88, 94, 114
Starks Warehouse Store, 92, **92,** 117
Stoch, Ron, 114
Streetcars, 55
Streets
  See Roads
Suburban Library System, 109, 111

T

Tanner, Francis, 22
Tanner, Henry, 22, 24, 34
Tanner, Ledore, 34, 49
Tanner, Lydia, 22
Tery, Ronald W., Rev., 103
Thatcher Avenue, 55
Thompson's Ice Cream & Bakery, **130**
Township Line Road, 27
Townships, 27
Trees, 3, 4
Truck farming, **56,** 57, 60, 66
Trump, J. Lloyd, 99

U

Union Ridge, 19, 49, 53
Union Ridge Cemetery
  See Cemeteries
Union Ridge School
  See Schools
Union Ridge, Village of, 85

V

Van Bergen
  See Bergen
Venture Limited
  See Ray Venture Limited

Venture Stores, Inc., **116**
Vietnam War, 111, **112**
Village Florist, 42
Vlchek, Edna, **133**

W

W. Bell & Co., **40**
Walgreen's, 84, **116**
War of 1812, 7-12, 20
Water tower, Norridge, **130**
Wells, William, 7-9
Wesleyan Church of Norridge
  See Churches
Westlawn Jewish Cemetery
  See Cemeteries
Wieboldt, W. A., 56
Wieboldt's, 56, 84, 122
Willas, Ray, **136**
William A. Lewis Women's Apparel, 84
Wilson Avenue, 22, 85
Wingert, Jacob, 26
Wingert, John, 26
Wingert, Maria, 26
Winnebago War of 1827, 21
Wisconsin, 26
Wisniewski, William, **111**
Wolanin, Toni, 109
Woolworth's, 84
World War One, 54, 55
World War Two, 64, 66, 67
Woyner, Linda, **110**
Wright Junior College, 122, **127**
WTTW (Channel 11, Chicago), 99

Z

Zabratanski, Medard, 119
Zion Evangelical Lutheran Church
  See Churches